Introduction

Cheaper than Chips is an interesting, informative collection of exclusive photographs, tips and facts about everything from antiques to bric-a-brac.

Many of the products in this book have been photographed on location at auctions, craft fairs and carboot sales. There are also a number of exclusive pictures including private collections that have never been photographed before.

The book has been put together using various sources and is designed to introduce you to the wonderful world of antiques and carboot sales, with handy hints and tips on what to look out for.

Prices will vary and are listed to provide a guide not a definitive reference. Prices are calculated using data collected from real auctions. All markets are subject to change, the prices quoted are correct at the time of going to print based upon the research compiled by the publisher. In any case in every auction situation, the piece is worth what the buyer is prepared to bid and any book on this subject cannot take into account the quality of your own items in terms of value.

Comments, questions and suggestions should be directed for the attention of the author to info@cheaperthanchips.com

The opinions in this book should not be relied upon for any reason. The publisher accepts no responsibility for loss or complaint caused by relying upon this book.

Although many of the items in this book are antiques, I would like to point out that the majority of the items featured are valued at less than £100 €140. And therefore will be of great demand to the small collector or investor, or the person just looking to de-clutter their own homes.

Along they way, with the aid of this book, we hope to provide an insight into the ever growing and popular world of the antique fair or carboot market. From items priced at as little as £5 €7 to £100's €100's, look at the many thousand of different objects and materials that are coming to the market place every day, objects such as china, toys, memorabilia, and many others.

Many of the items pictured have auction house stickers on them and it should be remembered that the valuation does not include any premium or tax that will be attached to that purchase.

Condition is crucial in any valuation and where other books usually show perfect items priced or estimated, this publication is more for the amateur who's goods have seen good use, and family heirlooms that for whatever reason you have decided to part with.

Finally I would just like to add; as an exciting hobby, or for anyone who has a collection large or small of collectable items, then this publication is a must. It is a very helpful aid to both the keen amateur, and those just starting off in this fast growing area. Far too many objects today are discarded unnecessarily, and a great many of these items lost forever. So please, next time you have a good clear out at home, be aware of objects of yesteryear, you would be amazed to see what some of these items sell for.

Very special thanks to all those who contributed to this book, you know who you are.

Good hunting!

At the time of going to print £1 = €1.4 to €1.5. This may fluctuate in value at any time.

GW00492890

Moorcroft history 1897 - present day

William Moorcroft was born in Burlem, Staffordshire. He trained to become an art teacher in South Kensington. In 1897 he was employed as a designer at Macintyre and Co., a Staffordshire earthenware manufacturer expanding into art and pottery.

At Macintyre's, Moorcroft's first designs were Aurelian (3 designs registered in 1898) and Dura ware, which was not signed. In 1897 he developed the first ornamental pieces, with Florian ware registered in 1898. He was entirely responsible for all the shapes of pottery and patterns developed carrying his name. All of these wares were hand made by skilled assistants, creating his designs in a raised slip.

In 1913 Moorcroft resigned to set up his own pottery and created the 'powder blue tableware' range. He also continued creating his other designs, with Florian ware continuing until 1965. Liberty were Moorcrofts most important customer in the 1900's, first appearing in the Liberty catalogue in 1913.

In the 1920's monochrome glazed wares were in fashion, followed in the 1930's by Moorcroft's distinctive Persian range. He also designed the flambé range, with endlessly varied designs, thought by many to be one of his greatest achievements.

In 1935 Moorcroft designed some more unusual shapes, a bacon plate, 3 and4 bar toast racks, lotion bottles for Austin Reed, square meat plates, jugs and inhalers for the war office and a range of named children's mugs.

Between 1934-35 he created over 50 designs featuring various grasses, berries, flowers, feathers, and trees fashioned in all colours.

Walter Moorcroft, William's son, joined the Company in 1935, and his first experimental designs started to come through in the late 1930's In 1945 Walter took over the business on his father's death. The style remained similar, but with Walter's more distinctive, personal designs emerging in the 1950's using more dramatic colours and exotic flowers depicted on the pottery.

In 1987 Walter's son John Moorcroft took over the business. The pattern range was further expanded. In 1991 Sally Tuffin became the principle designer with the individual painted colourings by Wendy Mason. Other designs are by Philip Richardson and various staff designs.

MARKS

There are several marks to look for printed or impressed on the base of the pottery, each for a different reason. Firstly there is the Moorcroft signature or initials. There are also retailer's marks (i.e. Liberties), design registration numbers and pattern or shape marks.

Paper labels with the factory marks printed on them were also widely used.

SIGNATURES

When working at Macintyres , William Moorcroft had a habit of signing all ware made under his control in his department, as a quality mark. His signature never meant he made or painted the piece himself. While working here he had several 'signatures'. W. Moorcroft des. WM des, or incised signatures or initials. These signatures are generally in green, but some other colours are used.

From 1945 Walter Moorcroft only signed new designs or important pieces in full. Other wares 5" and over or in diameter he would only initial. These initials were in blue, then in grey-green from 1959 to 1978. Then in 1978 the colour changed to brown and then again in 1981 it changed to green.

More recently the designer has used a full signature, especially when a piece has been designed with collectors in mind. Recently (1986 onward) the tube liners and paintresses have used painted letters of the alphabet and symbols to mark their work, also personal monograms.

RETAILER MARKS

There are some 20 of these noted, with liberties being the most important. Around 1906 many Florin pieces only carried the Moorcroft signature and Liberty's retail mark. Osler's were another big customer with the Hesperian range made for them and Shreve of San Francisco had many pieces painted for them.

FACTORY MARKS

There were two main styles, the factory name and signature, and the factory name, signature and royal mark from 1928.

During the Macintyre period there was always some form of printed factory mark, for the Florian ware, Butterfly ware and Hesperian ware. The Florian ware stopped its mark around 1905, replaced with the standard Macintyre monogram, backstamp, either on its own or with the retailer's mark.

Dating these marks can be difficult, with the design and decoration of the piece providing more clues to the date of manufacture. Sometimes important pieces

Cheaperthanchips.com

The Auction & CarBoot Guide

Thousands of pictures, descriptions and prices allow you to value items and compare collectables

Don't risk selling that family heirloom for a few pounds when it could be worth thousands!

The essential guide for buyers, sellers and budding collectors, Cheaper than Chips will save you time, energy and money! This easy to use, comprehensive price guide allows you to check out items before you buy or sell and give you a keen edge when haggling! Avoid expensive valuations and save time by becoming an expert yourself with Cheaper than Chips.

Cheaper than Chips will give you an insight into the world of antiques, collectables and bootsale bargains.

Visit our website:
www.CheaperthanChips.com
or write to:

Cheaper than Chips
PO Box 984
Hemel Hempstead
HP1 2ZU

Contains

The Auction&CarBootSale Guide

can be found with a date, or pieces produced when the factory moved from Washington to Colbridge between 1912 and 1914.

COMMEMORATIVE WARES

These were produced by both William and Walter Moorcroft, and tended to be adaptations of existing patterns with an inscription added, or a specially designed piece for an event or occasion. They could be anything from vases, bowls, jugs and pipe trays to complete tea services.

The distinctive characteristic is the style of hand lettering drawn in slip. The best examples of these are on Coronation mugs.

One of the earliest examples of this is a two handled mug made around 1902, inscribed with Christmas and New Year Greetings. There are also several private commissions from Mr. and Mrs. Lasenby (from Liberties)

Their is also a range of match holders with heraldic decoration for various Oxford and Cambridge Collages.

From the early 1900's to 1935 there was also a range of Motto ware, pieces with applied mottos in Latin and English.

Walter also manufactured his own range of commemorative pieces for the Coronation and the Jubilee of Queen Elizabeth II.

Other works have included popular limited edition (500) year plates from 1982-1986 then 1991-1993 and hand bells in 1983.

The Moorcroft Collectors club was established in 1987, which has its own magazine, collector's weekends, and open days with Auctions etc.

0096M Moorcroft vase
£210 €294

0098M Moorcroft Butterfly design vase **£180 €112**

0100M Moorcroft dish
£250 €350

0117M Moorcroft oblong dish
£60 €84

0113M Moorcroft tea-pot
£250 €350

0114M Small Moorcroft dish
£50 €70

0115M Moorcroft saucer
£35 €49

Cheaper than Chips

1. Moorcroft vase
   155mm high 6"
   £150 €210

2. Pot & cover
   £155 €220

3. Oval dish & cover
   £100 €140

4. Vase
   £155 €220

5. Vase
   £175 €245

6. Lamp base
   £155 €220

7. Early 20c vase
   £300 €420

8. Vase
   £145 €205

9. Signature on base
   of picture 8.

10. Signature on bottom of picture 11.

11. Cream jug
£115 €220

12. Signature on base
of pic 13.

13. Single candle stick
£1.60 €225

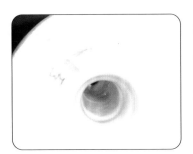

14. Signature example.

15. Small box & cover
£110 €155

16. Signature on small
box.

17. Vase
£140 €196

18. Signature of pic 17.

19. Vase
£160 €225

Cheaper than Chips

20. Signature picture 21

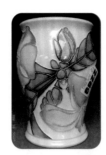

21. Vase
£145 €205

22. Vase
£190 €266

23. Signature of picture 22.

24. Small vase
£120 €170

LM08. The Leonardo collection
'Man and his dog'
£15 €21

26. Vase
£130 €180

27. Tea cup & saucer
£110 €155

28. Small vase
£130 €180

29. Vase 10" 250mm **£210 €300**

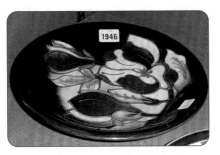

30. Candle stick 6" 150mm **£80 €110**

31. Plate approx.10" 250mm **£140 €200**

32. Plate approx.10" 250mm **£160 €225**

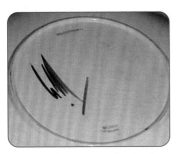

33. Signature on back of picture 32.

34. Small vase 5" 130mm **£110 €155**

35. Vase 11" 300mm **£195 €275**

36. Vase 12" 300mm **£150 €210**

37. Window/desk display plaque **£130 €180**

38. Minature vase 4" 100mm **£75 €105**

Cheaper than Chips

39. Vase
£150 €210

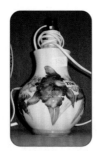

40. Lamp
£200 €280

41. Pot 5" 120mm
£110 €155

HY32. Homepride salt, pepper
& spice holders
£5 €7 each

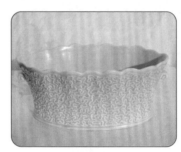

HY33. Sylvac vase
pattern. 2301
£20 €28

HY43. China
posy holder
£5 €7

HY46. Modern
'Winnie the Pooh' bear
£5 €7

HY44. 3 Badminton racquets
circa 1960
£30 €42

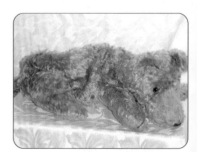

HY45. Merrythought nightie
holder circa 1950
£60 €84

550. Pair of plated vases **£40 €56**

551. Four bottle condiment **£30 €42**

552. Large Victorian tea pot **£150 €210**

553. Four silver plated figures **£40 €56**

554. Plated hot water jug **£30 €42**

555. Art Deco cut glass cocktail jug **£100 €140**

556. Silver-plated tea pot **£30 €42**

557. Outside of cutlery box picture 558.

558. Cutlery box and contents **£60 €84**

559. Cannon **£20 €28**

563. Hornby train **£100 €140**

Royal Doulton figures

The history of Royal Doulton dates back to 1815 when John Doulton, a journeyman called Watts and a widow by the name of Jones were established at Vauxhall opposite the gate of the famous Vauxhall pleasure gardens, the haunt of the fashionable of the 19th century.

Although the widow Jones disappeared from the scene shortly afterwards, Watts and Doulton continued until 1853 when Mr Watts retired. John's son Henry joined the firm in 1835 and this expanded the business rapidly.

By this time the company had moved to Lambeth High Street. This was later to become known as the famous Lambeth pottery. Henry Doulton began to pursue more artistic designs, with John carrying on the now already famous lines of general stoneware, such as ginger beer bottles and chemical and industrial ceramics, which are used around the world.

By the 1800's the company had grown to over 300 employees producing sculptures, decorative vases and figures for an eager Victorian market, under the guidance of George Tinworth who joined the company in 1867. The medium he used is known as salt glaze stoneware.

Tinworth's colleague John Broad also used this material as well as terracotta to produce portraits, military figures and female studies in classical style.

The last figure maker of note at Lambeth was Leslie Harradine who made a number of slip cat figures in small editions. Some of these were reintroduced in the 1920's including the famous Dickens characters.

These were made at Doulton's other factory in Burslem, Stoke on Trent in the world famous Harry Nixon (HN) collection. HN was in charge of the new figure painting department, and in the 20's and 30's saw a new age of figure painters emerging, notably Percy Curnock.

The Second World War limited the production of the figurines with many of the artists and workers going off to war, and pretty much only luxury goods were produced for export.

After the Second World War, not surprisingly the collection was rationalised, and the 1920's style and colour effect began to give way to more commercial sense.

However, the idea was revived during the 1980's initially for special events, when a new colouring way of 'wistful' (HN2472) was introduced.

BACK STAMPS, DATING AND MARKS

Most common is the Lion standing on a crown, this was used ever since Royal Doulton were awarded the Royal warrant in 1901. Three years after its founder Henry Doulton died in 1897. He was however the first potter ever to be given a knighthood by Queen Victoria in 1887.

Before 1901 the mark was of a different style crown and the words 'Doulton Burslem England'. This mark is found mostly on the vellum figures made by Charles Noke in the 1890's.

The words 'Made in England' were added around the 1920's as from 1902-1922. Just the word England was used. These were printed or impressed on the bottom. These are easily dated for collectors.

E.G A number by the side of the crown '1' stands for 1928, '2' 1929, etc. up to 1954.

The HN number is also particularly important as all designs were in HN number order from their catalogue. The painters very occasionally omitted this, so it is now stamped on along with the figure's name and copyright information.

SECONDS

Although 'seconds were not the available to the public, employees of the company could purchase them at special sales. They are clearly marked, however, with either a drill hole on the lion or a score line through the backstamp or signature. These do come onto the market so buyers beware the price of a perfect piece is considerably more than a second.

TIPS

Always try to acquire the certificate issued with the figure; these are not supplied usually to seconds. It would be impossible to show all the Doulton range, they have been awarded hundreds of awards from around the world, virtually since they began. Notably their first to achieve high acclaim was at the Paris exhibition 1867.

COLLECTING

There is no shortage of reference books for collectors of Doulton and most auction houses have a steady flow of pieces so wide has the range been, we have photographed, mostly items of the last twenty to thirty years. We think you will have a better chance of finding some of these, however, once you are familiar with the HN marks on the figures, or D marks on the character jugs E.G (D6753) Anne of Cleeves, although not a terribly valuable piece is a typical example. Also look out for a range of miniatures (M series) average height 4" or 10cm. If you come across any of these it might well be worth a trip to your local library. They range in price from £40 to £1000, e.g. M89 Oliver Twist 4¼" or 10.8cm issued 1939-1983 £40. Obviously this subject is quite common. Where as M17, M18, M19 and M20 shepherd and shepherdess all 3¾" 9.5cm issued 1932-1938 £1500 each!!

42. Melanie
£100 €140

43. Sunday Best
£80 €112

44. Hilary
£90 €126

45. Little Ballerina & Penny
£40 each €55

46. Clarissa
£95 €133

47. Monica (miniature)
£40 €55

48. Arnold Bennett
£90 €126

49. Tobacco jar, salt glazed
£30 €42

50. Presentation bowl 225mm
£50 €70

51. Thoughts for you
£90 €126

Cheaper than Chips

52. Victoria
£90 €126

53. Fair lady
£90 €126

54. Allison
£90 €126

55. Top of the hill
£90 €126

56. Stephanie
£90 €126

57. Part tea set, norfolk
pattern **£95 €133**

58. John Barleycorn character
jug **£50 €70**

59. Farmer John
£50 €70

60. Farmer John base

61. Miniatures: Apothecary & Mine Host
£45 €63 each

62. Vases (pair)
£80 €112

63. White glazed
toothless gran **£35 €49**

64. George Washington
£65 €90

65. Robin Hood
£55 €77

66. Scaramouche
£65 €90

67. Beefeater & Long John Silver
£60 €85 each

68. American Indian
£55 €77

69. The Lawyer
£50 €70

70. The Artful Dodger
(series plate) **£50 €70**

Cheaper than Chips

71. Winsome
£75 €105

72. Amy & Diane
£90 €126

73. SouthernBelle & First Dance
£90 €126

74. Laura
£90 €126

75. Becky
£90 €126

76. Sweet Violets
£80 €112

77. Osprey whisky flask
225mm **£50 €70**

LM21. Royal Doulton fig. of
the year 2000 'Rachel'
£140 €196

79. Stoneware hunting jug
£50 €70

80. The Blacksmith
£60 €85

81 Loretta
£90 €126

82. Chloe & Ashley & Diane
£90 €126 each

83. Fragrance
£90 €126

85. Desperate Dan &
George Washington £60 €85

86. Anne of Cleves & Athos
£60 €85

84. For You
£90 €126

87. Merlin
£65 €90

LM15. Christmas Day 2000,
HN4242
£100 €140

Top Tips

Antique markets and fairs are great for collectors but may not be the best place to find a bargain if you are a beginner. Over the next few pages you will find handy hints and tips to get you started.

CHECK THEM OUT FIRST

If you are considering clearing the clutter from your life. (Near relatives not included) then take some time to examine which items should go where. Old furniture and valuable items, should be either sent for Auction or sold in the local paper. With the help of this book, hopefully, the mistakes of the amateur can be reduced. For the more sought after items, and collectibles you should consider the Internet. Internet sites can also accurately value your items, just like selling a car, check out what every one else is selling that item for then set your price, sites like E-BAY are a good starting place.

Once you have sorted all your items, it's time to locate a venue.

If you have sorted out maybe 20 items for Auction then visit some auction houses first. Ask some questions, take a list of your articles, or better still some photographs to your local auction house, they will usually be able to save you some time and money, in transportation costs, for items they consider not viable for sale, usually under £20.

Other items such as bric-a-brac, china, porcelaine, clothes and household items, look up a good carboot sale. Go along and check it out, look at their set up. What do you need, how many stalls are there, is it busy, what sort of tables are available, must I bring my own? Are there any amenities, toilets, hot drinks, sheltering on wet days?. Once you have decided, its time for action. Pick your day, load up your car the night before as the early bird catches the worm; this also ensures you have not left anything behind in the last minute rush.

ONCE YOU'RE THERE

Most carboot sales have a different time to arrive for buyers and sellers. This is because, fortunately over the years they have learned by their mistakes, cars and people in fields generally do not mix well. Also buyers rummaging through your boxes whilst you attempt to set up is not a good idea, breakages and theft are the worst possible start to a day at the carboot sale.

So take your time, put your fewer valuables out first, leaving room for more valuable items at the back of your table. Don't let people help you, take your time, don't sell any item until your ready.

BE FRIENDLY

I go to many fairs and markets, and just like any retail outlet you need to project yourself, and your wares. Too often I see people sitting there almost indifferent to their potential buyers. Busy yourself around your stall, cleaning re-arranging items, smile, try to catch their eye, try to enlist help, partners, children; you may also have to visit the toilet, get to know the people around you. Be as helpful as possible, try to think ahead, what's the weather forecast, maybe you could sell a few old umbrellas, or plastic Macs. Have some polythene sheeting at hand to quickly cover your stall in the event of a shower. Bring hot food and drinks, these will perk you up.

BEST WARES OUT EARLY

If you are considering attending your first carboot sale, then try to follow these simple tips for best results. Always get there early. If it says sellers from 7am, then be there by 6.45, try to get a stall in the first room, or near the entrance. Get your best pieces out at the front of your table, as most collectors will be attracted if other quality items are on view. Remember to have plenty of change, the last thing you need with 2 or 3 people looking at items on your stall, is to have to go off in search of change, or worse still let an item go for 50p less than you wanted because you don't have any.

CHARITY SHOPS

Whilst most items of any value are sorted by people in the know and passed onto collectors or dealers, you may still find the odd item, or gem sitting on the shelf. I know most dealers or collectors visit charity shops especially in affluent areas, I have picked up many items in the past, and made over 200%-300% profit in days.

LOCAL PAPERS

Look for information on sales, items for sale under £50. Jumble sales, school fetes etc. There are literally thousands of these sales going on in the spring and summer as schools and clubs gear up their fund raising activities. You can usually get a table quite easily at these functions, for a small donation and move a lot of smaller items that you may have amassed. I recently gave two boxes full of bric-a-brac to my father in law, for the bowls club carboot sale. I considered the contents mostly junk with just a few items included to make it interesting. He later phoned me to thank me, they sold virtually everything for £160.

SPRING CLEANING

Just after the spring-cleaning season begins the whole carboot sale market sees a boost. What some see as junk may be valuable or just cheap to others. Ask yourself this, is it worth taking items to the rubbish tip, many for recycling. When you could just as easily give up a few hours on a Sunday and go to a sale and recycle your items there; after all they will not give you any money at the tip.

QUALITY WORKMANSHIP

Whatever you buy try to stick to three basic tips,

1. Is it well made, or does it have a unique quality? Even things like old perfume bottles are very collectable today because the packaging has been designed to sell the product it contains.

2. Marks. Many quality items have the maker's name stamped or printed on them. Also, these items may have been patented, because at the time it was unique or new, get to know a few marks, you will be surprised how many single china or pottery items go unsold, many valuable, because the buyers are not familiar with the factory marks.

3. Collectables are usually just that, collectable, because they are of a high quality, maybe hand decorated, or engraved or part of a set, never over look that single piece of china that maybe hand painted, or decorated with gold leaf. Take it home and do a little research on it, you may be surprised. If it turns out to be less than you originally though, you can always re-sell it.

MONEY - HAGGLE, BARGAIN

Always price your items a little over, as it is a rare that buyers will pay the full asking price for your wares at a carboot sale. People love a bargain if something is priced at £12 and they get it for £8, this will put a spring in their step. Be firm but friendly, teach yourself a few one-liners that will put the potential buyer at ease, like 'Its been in the family for years and I could not possibly let it go for that'.

Stories of hardship and woe will enter a funny side to the negotiations and break the ice. Offer them a bag to put it in at no extra cost. If people are at your table, and laughter can be heard others will come over to see what the hilarity is all about. Remember this important rule. People do not like at anytime to be pressurised into a sale, and like to browse. This is easier for them to do if people are already at your stall. It gives them more time to look around your table if you're busy, and if something takes their eye they will have more time to examine the piece without pressure. They may even see something else they like as well, then you have two sales.

CARRIER BAGS

Remember to take a lot of carrier bags with you to any carboot sale as most buyers will expect them, put things like dinner & tea sets in a strong box and lots of soft packaging. This allows the buyer to transport them home safely. Offer to look after the box until the buyers have finished browsing the rest of the market, (Always get the money first, when doing this, for obvious reasons)

Don't expect to become an Antique dealer overnight Many visitors who arrive early for carboot sales may be dealers, and this will be your most testing time; what with setting up your stall, getting settled, the anxiety of the crowd waiting to come in, etc. They will drive the hardest for the bargains - even telling you that it may be a copy, or it's a second. Or buy something of virtually no value then try to marry it in with a second item greatly reduced, stick to your guns, if something you are selling is valued for £20 never let it go for less than £15 even if they have already bought items. This sleeper may have been what they have been after all along. It's tough at the time but its better to stick to your guns and maximize your profits at the expense of theirs. Odds on they will still take it.

WHAT CAN I SELL AT A CARBOOT SALE?

Virtually anything, but please be sensible, tobacco or alcoholic products may seem attractive at first glance, but Customs & Excise rules apply - and they do visit sites on a regular basis - you have been warned.

Foam furniture i.e. old chairs and settees, are covered by the law, and fire regulations on many of these items are strict, which is why so many Auction houses refuse to Auction them, so its off to the rubbish tip with these I'm afraid.

Live stock is also a not a good idea, this may cause arguments to break out over the conditions these creatures are kept in. And the conditions they may have come from will almost certainly be doubtful, if you have kittens or puppies you wish to sell, place the add in your local newsagents' window.

Fire arms either replica or not, are also on the not desired list, for obvious reasons.

Chemicals, drugs etc. Although most gardening products do appear at carboot sales if you intend selling these items please ensure that they are in date, and safely packaged for transporting. If very old or poisonous please take these items to your local tip for proper disposal. Never attempt to resell any pharmaceutical products.

Electrical goods are not good either, unless you can guarantee personally that they are in perfect working order, even then they rarely sell, so try your local paper for all electrical or white goods.

There are others more obscure but the sensible approach is usually the right one, if it's dangerous, or in poor condition, or may harm the new owner, then do not attempt to re-sell any item.

Cheaper than Chips

88. Two 1930's wooden painted boxes **£40 €56**

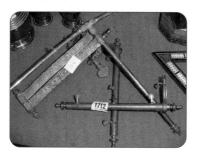

89. 19c. brass face screen crane & two curtain mounts **£50 €70**

90. Brass/copper ewer & 2 brass match pots **£25 €35**

91. Cribbage score board wood/ivory **£30 €42**

92. Watch box & inlaid octagonal box **£35 €49**

93. Bronze figure table lamp **£40 €56**

94. Green onyx mantel clock **£45 €63**

95. Patinated metal photo frame **£40 €56**

96. Brass cased compass **£45 €63**

Top Tips

Onyx in it's natural colour ranges from black through to white with brown running through it. However it was very easy to dye and dyed green Onyx is very popular as shown in picture 94.

570. Samovar
£75 €105

Cheaper than Chips

Money Boxes...

...as we know have been around for centuries, in one shape or another, which probably explains their popularity as collectors' items. In the age of the credit card these items are more likely to become even more collectable.

571. Electric guitar
£150 €210

572. Bellows
£40 €56

573. Copper vessel
£30 €42

574. Two Victorian lanterns **£50 €70**

575. Jam pan
£20 €28

576. Large brass jam pan
£40 €56

577. Art Deco coal bucket
£70 €98

581. Two spelter figures **£20 €28**

578. Bronze figure of a dog and puppies **£180 €252**

579. Queen's dolls house moneybox **£30 €42**

580. Edwardian inlaid clock by Asprey & Co. **£100 €140**

Cheaper than Chips

582. Bronze figure of a
young girl **£150** €**210**

583. Glass bowl on spelter
stand **£40** €**56**

584. Chinoiserie cased clock
£40 €**56**

585. Copper kettle
£40 €**56**

586. Copper kettle
£30 €**42**

587. Victorian slate mantel
clock **£50** €**70**

588. Microscope in box
£100 €**140**

589. Inside of picture 588.

590. Two Spelter figures
£40 €**56**

591. Georgian bed pan
£30 €**42**

592. Coffin shaped puzzle box & jewellery box **£60 £30 €84 €42**

593. Georgian mahogany tea caddy **£80 €112**

594. Victorian Epergne and oriental brass vase **£40 each €56 each**

595. Lacquered box **£30 €42**

596. Burr walnut two-compartment caddy **£60 €84**

597. Noddy foam toy **£20 €28**

598. Pair of blue and white vases **£100 €140**

599. Painted movie glass vase **£30 €42**

600. Pair of Satsuma vases **£100 €140**

601. Pair of blue and white Royal Bonne vases **£100 €140**

602. Moorcroft vase **£210 €294**

Cheaper than Chips

98. Carved & painted
ink box **£35 €49**

99. Pair brass fire tongs **£10 €14**

100. French gilt metal jardiniere
£45 €63

97. Green patinated
bronzed figure
£45 €63

101. Walnut stationary box
£80 €112

102. Picture of inside pic 101.

103. Oriental carved soap
stone sculpture **£50 €70**

Soapstone

(magnesium silicate) is a soft stone material often used for carving and was especially used for oriental works in a range of colours including white, red and mottled green. Please see picture 103.

104. Box set of chemical balance weights **£50 €70**

603. Chinese blue & white vase and cover **£50 €70**

604. Frilled glass vase **£20 €28**

605. Majolica dish **£100 €140**

606. Bretby vase **£100 €140**

607. Poole Pottery vase **£45 €63**

608. Continental figure group **£50 €70**

609. Wade Toucan figure **£42 €59**

610. Royal Copenhagen "Guardian Angel" plaques **£100 €140**

611. Two oriental plates **£40 €56**

Cheaper than Chips

105. Picture of inner pic 104.

107. Late Victorian ebonised mantel clock **£60** €**85**

110. Pair of handcuffs & manacles **£45** €**63**

108. Art deco period walnut mantel clock **£80** €**112**

111. Miniature grand piano **£60** €**85**

106. Smiths motor car clock **£30** €**42**

109. Dagger & sheath **£40** €**56**

612. Moorcroft bowl and cover **£110** €154

613. Poole Pottery vase **£80** €112

614. Three cut glass items **£30** €42

617. Two slip ware dishes **£45** €63

615. Pinnacle posy **£15** €21

616. Oval Moorcroft bowl **£115** €161

618. Pair of coloured vases **£80** €112

619. Moorcroft vase **£45** €63

LM73. Robertson's Golly musicians group 1970 **£70** €98

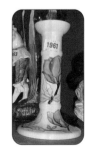

621. Moorcroft candle stick **£80** €112

Cheaper than Chips

622. Pair of figural vases
£250 €350

LM27. Royal Doulton fig. of the year 'Sarah' **£140 €196**

624. Cloisonné vase **£35 €49**

625. Staffordshire figure of a lion **£80 €112**

626. Moorcroft plate **£135 €189**

627. Four continental menu holders **£15 €21**

628. Hammersley coffee pot and other items **£40 €56**

629. Moorcroft plate **£155 €217**

630. Base of picture 629.

Waterford Crystal

The most famous of Irish glass makers since the early part of the 18th Century, producing many thousands of useful and beautifully crafted pieces, to be found in any top ten list of collectables.

631. Art Deco style continental coffee set **£20 €28**

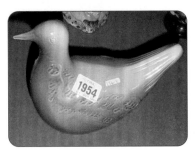

632. Bird figure **£28 €39**

634. Scottish glass jug **£50 €70**

633. Copper lustre jug & metal ware vase **£35 £10 €49 €14**

635. Royal Doulton Lambeth silicone jardiniere **£50 €70**

636. Doulton Lambeth silicone jardiniere **£50 €70**

637. Lladro figure group 'Boy with a dog' **£75 €105**

638. Amber glass jug and plate **£20 €28**

639. Waterford crystal water jug **£35 €49**

640. Tea pot etc. **£40 €56**

Cheaper than Chips

641. Pair of oriental vases **£30** €42

642. Pair staffordshire figures of Penholdes **£50** €70

643. Lladro figure of a girl with a candle **£40** €56

645. Series of nine water birds plates **£100** €140

644. Continental pottery plaque **£40** €56

646. Three graduated Meat plates **£75** €105

647. Poole Pottery vase **£25** €35

LM28. Royal Doulton 'Millennium Celebration' **£140** €196

649. Two 1960's vases **£40** €56

Tazza...

...is a name given to a tray or dish mounted upon a pedestal, see picture 121.

Although this is quite a plain example they can be made from glass, china, wood, copper or brass.

112. 19c. cut glass Tazza on stand **£35** €**49**

113. Two painted ostrich eggs on stand **£30** €**42**

114. 19c brass cased barometer **£40** €**56**

115. Late 19c. oriental brass box **£40** €**56**

116. Picture of inner pic 115.

117. 4 oriental measuring pots **£30** €**42**

118. Oriental Senza & stand **£75** €**105**

119. 19c. Chinese dancing figure **£35** €**49**

120. Oriental pot cover & stand **£25** €**35**

121. Late 19c. bronze Tazza **£80** €**112**

Cheaper than Chips

650. Royal Doulton character jug 'Old Salt' **£45** €63

652. Two crackle glass items **£40** €56

653. Lladro figure 'Group of geese' **£45** €63

655. Five crackle glass items **£40** e56

651. Painted lilac opaque glass vase **£50** €70

654. Poole Pottery dish **£35** €49

657. Lladro figure group 'Little girl and dogs' **£75** €105

656. Copeland Spode meat dish and three plates **£40** €56

658. Beswick figure of a horse **£39** €55

Willow pattern

The Willow Pattern is thought to have been designed by Englishman Thomas Minton and not a Chinese imported idea. He is thought to have invented the pattern whilst working for Thomas Turner who used it on his own porcelain, better known as Salopian. Minton went on to develop his own pottery from 1970 and widely used the transfer printed blue colour. On pottery however, it was copied by many throughout the 1800's.

(Continued on Page 33)

659. Lladro figure of a seagull **£50 €70**

It was very commonly used to decorate earthenware items for the table.

Early earthenware was in cobalt and even black. Reds, purples or brown are normally attributed to the Victorian era. Particularly Mason ironstone and Spode from 1813. Ironstone was extremely hard and cheap to produce although probably not the most decorative example it was very durable and early examples still survive.

660. Poole Pottery vase **£80 €112**

661. Two blue and white willow patterned meat dishes **£40 €56**

662. Royal Doulton jardiniere **£60 €84**

663. Royal Worcester cake serving plate **£30 €42**

664. Brass coal scuttle **£30 €42**

665. Two brass fire dogs **£50 €70**

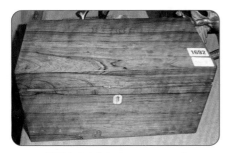

666. Late Victorian rosewood tea caddie **£80 €112**

667. Inside of picture 666.

668. Brass figure 'The discus thrower' **£20 €28**

Cheaper than Chips

669. Brass figure of St. George & Dragon **£85** €**119**

670. Rosewood needle work box **£40** €**56**

671. Victorian walnut writing slope **£80** €**112**

674. Silver plated panel of Luis Waller **£30** €**42**

672. Ceramic clock **£50** €**70**

673. Brass Cannon **£20** €**28**

675. Bronze mantel clock **£150** €**210**

676. Horn **£25** €**35**

677. Three bottle tantalus **£200** €**280**

678. Victorian walnut cased mantel clock **£50** €**70**

Cheaper than Chips

Book Ends...

...are sadly becoming almost obsolete in the modern world, but good old or well fashioned ones are still worth looking out for.

679. Oriental carved wooden figure
£40 €56

680. Fish kettle
£30 €42

681. Two fire dogs
£20 €28

684. Set scale and weights
£15 €21

682. Copper and brass coal bucket **£130 €182**

683. Copper coal scuttle
£25 €35

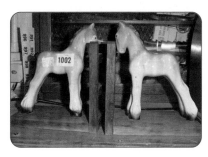

685. Pair 'Foal' book ends
£12 €17

686. Radio
£30 €42

687. Teapot
£12 €17

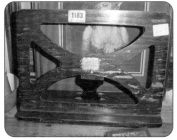

689. Music desk **£15 €21**

Cheaper than Chips

688. Mantel clock
£35 €49

690. Roberts radio
£10 €14

691. Murphy radio
£20 €28

692. Moorland jug / Lorna Bailey 'Cat' figure &
Moorland tea pot **£25 £40 £38 €35 €56 €53**

693. Lorna Bailey bird
£70 €98

694. Moorland jug
£30 €42

695. Magnifying glass / Moorland jug
and Lorna Bailey 'Cat' figure
£10 £30 £45 €14 €42 €63

696. Lorna Bailey tea pot
£40 €56

697. Set of white painted scales
and weights **£40 €56**

Radios

Radios are probably the most important invention of all time. No other medium could capture the imagination of the world's population in an instant. It brought music, theatre and news. Many may say that television should have this accolade but to the masses throughout the 20th Century radio was able to capture the hearts and minds of whole nations instantly from early crystal sets in wooden boxes, then bake light and plastic transistors. No household in the modern world is without one.

717. Mantel clock
£30 €42

716. Toby jug and jug
£15 £10 €21 €14

718. Pot pourri and cover
£40 €56

719. H. Samuel chiming
mantel clock **£40 €56**

720. Mantel clock
£15 €21

721. Wind up gramophone
£80 €112

722. Old wind up
gramophone **£80 €112**

723. Inside of
picture 722.

724. Wireless
£25 €35

Cheaper than Chips

725. Set of scales and weights **£15 €21**

726. Part Copeland Spode dinner service **£40 €56**

727. Picnic set **£20 €28**

728. Inside of picture 727.

729. Wireless **£20 €28**

730. Tin car **£20 €28**

731. Old Badminton set **£30 €42**

732. Carved wood Elephant stand **£10 €14**

733. Old cash register **£20 €28**

Toys

Hornby was one of the great toy makers of all time. Look out for pieces from the 1940's and 1950's. If you can get them from an auction the price you will pay wil be a good guide to their actua value. They can increase by a much as 10 - 15% a year!

734. Small wooden carriage **£10** €**14**

735.RAC sign **£20** €**28**

737.1980's Dinky toy **£10** €**14**

736. Old television **£20** €**28**

738. Soup tureen **£20** €**28**

739.1970's One-arm Bandit, electric **£50** €**70**

LM74. Robertson's Golly musicians group 1970 **£70** €**98**

741. Rosewood & pearl inlaid needlework box **£45** €**63**

742. Late Victorian brass perpetual day calender **£40** €**56**

743. Boxed brass chemical balance **£30** €**42**

Cheaper than Chips

744. Gurkha soldier figure, recumbent lion **£60** €84

745. Carved wood two bottle ink stand **£45** €63

746. Late Victorian walnut mantel clock **£120** €168

747. Crackle glass centre piece with three dancing figures **£30** €42

748. French copper mantel clock **£100** €140

749. Quartz mantel clock, blue glass cigarette box **£35** €49

LM72. Belleek vase brown back stamps **£20** €28

752. Hondo guitar/ tuner/ book **£100** €140

751. Bronzed figure group of a dog and pups **£100** €140

753. Carved wood figure of Madonna **£25** €28

754. Early 19c. Copper urn on stand **£45** €63

755. Copper kettle **£25** €35

Lustre Ware

Lustre is basically a metallic film from such substances as the oxides of gold or platinum. These could be sprayed onto virtually any item copper, porcelain or pottery. The silver colour is obtained from platinum on a white or cream base, pink from gold on a similar body colour and copper from gold on a red body. A thin film of metallic glaze on porcelain or earthenware could very cheaply produce imitation copper or silver effects. The method of application varied from spraying on items to give a full colour effect or brush painted on to highlight bands, reliefs, scrolls on raised decorative patterns or flowers etc.

706. 1960s Cutlery box
£30 €42

707. A quantity of commemorative items
£20 €28

708. Zither
£50 €70

710. Musical instrument
£15 €21

711. Copper kettle
£20 €28

712. Old telephone
£40 €56

709. Oriental vase
£30 €42

714. Samovar
£40 €56

715. Two copper Lustre items **£25 €28**

713. Old bus ticket machine
£12 €17

Cheaper than Chips

765. Walnut case mantel clock **£40** €56

766. Banjo **£35** €49

767. Oriental bronze vase **£60** €84

768. Plate **£32** €45

770. Pair of blue & white Royal Bonn vases **£80** €112

769. Continental Faience bowl **£35** €49

771. Macintyre jug **£260** €364

772. Bretby jug **£15** €21

773. Coloured glass vase ewer **£20** €28

774. Cut glass liqueur decanter & stopper **£30** €42

775. Royal Worcester tureen base **£40** €56

Labels

Items marked with A/F (as found) or A/S (as seen) are items offered for sale despite a fault such as a crack or chip. It may also indicate the piece has been restored.

It may still be a collectable item with a high value, but be aware that it will be valued at the less than perfect end of the price scale.

42

776. Seven green wine glasses
£40 €56

777. Royal Doulton jug 'Frankenstein' monster **£52 €73**

778. Pair Royal Doulton character jugs **£165 €231**

779. Three blue glass decanters and two stoppers **£50 €70**

781. Novelty Carlton ware tea pot and jug **£40 €56**

782. Fielding and Co. Jardiniere **£20 €28**

783. Pair of vases **£40 €56**

780. Coalport figure **£35 €49**

784. Wedgewood tea pot **£35 €49**

785. Royal Worcester tureen, cover and gravy pot **£40 €56**

Cheaper than Chips

756. Late 19c. French bronze figure of a lady **£750** €**1050**

757. Brass magnifying glass **£20** €**28**

758. Walnut cased, brass mounted mantel clock by Hughes of London **£70** €**98**

759. 1960's Smiths chime clock **£15** €**21**

760. Oriental carved wood and bone inlaid box **£35** €**49**

761. Two branch wall sconce **£35** €**49**

762. Binoculars **£10** €**14**

763. Inlaid mahogany mantel clock **£50** €**70**

764. Oak mantel clock **£40** €**56**

533. Royal Doulton sugar box
and cover **£50 €70**

534. Three Beswick
birds **£30 €42**

535. Pair of Royal Doulton
vases **£60 €84**

536. Art Deco glass
decanter **£20 €28**

537. China pepper and salt
clowns **£10 €14**

538. Two Royal Doulton figures
from 101 Dalmations
£75 €105

540. Japanese pepper, salt &
butter dish with cover
£15 €21

539. Two cow creamers
£80 €112

541. Three Beswick birds
£30 €42

Cheaper than Chips

815. Royal Doulton Berkshire pattern part dinner service **£45 €63**

816. 19c. Blue and white meat dish **£40 €56**

817. Canteen of cutlery **£40 €56**

818. Inside of picture 817.

819. Canteen of cutlery **£40 €56**

820. Inside of picture 819.

821. Sylvac Corgi mournful puppy; Terrier **£80 €112**

822. 19c. Royal Doulton figure **£60 €84**

823. Royal Doulton figures 'Adrienne' & 'Finishing Touch' **£75 each €105 each**

SylvaC

Founded in 1894 by William Shaw & William Copestake the SylvaC potteries produced thousands of house hold items and "fancies" for nearly 100 years until it ceased trading in 1982. At this time many of the designs and records for the company were lost, and new and rare pieces occasionally surface, so it is worth looking out for them as they can be very valuable, as well as some of the most collectable.

LM30. Royal Doulton classic
'Francesca' Ltd. 80/2500
£150 €210

LM31. Base of
'Francesca'
pic LM30.

826. Pair of continental porcelain
figures & Dresden figure
£40 each €56 each

827. Moorcroft vase
£120 €168

828. Royal Doulton figure
Amanda **£30 €42**

829. Royal Doulton figure 'Spring
Morning' and a Royal Doulton
'Osprey' flask **£75 £42 €105 €59**

830. Framed pot lid
£40 €56

831. Royal Doulton small character
jug, Cooper and Goss jug
£42 £40 €59 €56

832. Pair of continental figures,
Fruit Sellers **£50 €70**

833. Continental
fairing **£15 €21**

Wade Pottery 1867 - present day

Wade ceramics LTD originally consisted of a number of potteries, which were run by either members of, or friends of the Wade family.

These various factories eventually amalgamated in 1958 to form The Wade Group of Potteries Ltd.

The companies best well known before this amalgamation were John Wade and Co., (1867); Wade and Co., (1887); J & W Wade & Co., (1891); Wade Heath & Co., (1927); George Wade & Son (1927) and AJ Wade LTD (1927).

The most recent of the Wade names is Wade (PDM) LTD, the PDM standing for Point of sale Marketing Distribution.

In the early days Wade potteries were better known for their manufacture of industrial ceramics, used in the textile industry, also supplying the first burners for domestic gas lighting.

GEORGE WADE & SON LTD - THE FIRST FIGURINES

The expansion into figurines came about in the late 1920's, when George Wade and son LTD produced a range of modestly priced decorative figures. Jessica Van Hallen, a talented designer was brought in as the head designer for the Wade Company. A lot of her designs were of Art Deco appearance, and are very hard to find in mint condition, therefore highly sought after by collectors. These earthenware figures and wall masks had a cellulose finish, unfortunately this turned yellow, disintegrating and peeling away from the figure. This process was discontinued in the late 1930's, and in 1935 a new underglaze was introduced which fared better, and the factory continued to produce both old and new designs.

Designs included a range of small figurines, mostly named ladies and girls, and a few animals. The exact numbers produced are not known.

The marks on these figures tended to read 'WADE figures made in England,' with a leaping deer pictured over the writing, and the name of the figure. The animals tended to be marked 'Wade Made in England', but some had no marks at all.

In 1939 Faust Lang, a talented wood carver was employed to carve animal shapes, these were passed to the mold makers who made master molds for slip cast production. These pieces were marketed prior to WW1, then a small amount in the 1940's. Most of these pieces were marked Wade England.

FLOWERS 1930-39

This range of decorative ware are very hard to find in mint condition, and carry mainly handwritten marks with a number and name.Other series produced were the Tinker, tailor soldier sets, Goldilocks, Butcher, baker, candlestick maker and various nursery rhyme themes.

WADE HEATH & CO. ANIMALS 1937-1950'S

This Wade Company expanded the animal figures with both comic and realistic animal figures. In the late 1950's they produced a very popular animal set comprising of a puppy, miniature deer, Dartmoor ponies, foals and a rabbit.

In the late 1950's a range of novelty figures were produced, including the Drum box series, Noddy figures, Child studies, The Bisto Kids range and Mabel Lucie Attwell characters.

Later in 1959 the range of Hannah Barbera cartoon characters were introduced including the likes of Yogi Bear and Mr. Jinks.

WADE GROUP OF COMPANIES LTD - WHIMSIES 1959-1984

One of the names most synonymous with Wade, these little animal figures were first produced in 1959. They were ten sets of 5 pieces manufactured in limited quantities, at about one yearly interval. The first 5 sets made in even lesser quantities than the last 5. The very first set consisted of a leaping fawn, horse, squirrel, spaniel and poodle. The last 5 sets were more 'themed', i.e. polar, North American animals, farm animals, zoo and pedigree dogs.

New lines of 'Whimsies' were introduced again in 1971 and withdrawn in 1984. These pieces were sold individually or in boxed sets. The range has extended over the years to a complete range of some 60 pieces, each set of 5 coming in a different colour box.

DISNEY 1961-1965

These figures marked 'Wade copyright Walt Disney Productions made in England', included money boxes which came in sets of 5.

In the mid 1960's the demand for the small decorative pieces almost ceased and Wade looked into other areas of expansion. They a to do a lot more 'contract' orders around the 1970's. This included work for breweries, distilleries and tobacco manufacturers, making such things as ashtrays, promotional items;

whisky jugs and 'give aways' to go in crackers. One of the biggest promotions was for Brooke Bond tea, where a collection of 60 different miniature animal figures were given away in the Red Rose Tea promotion in Canada, which ceased in 1979. Wade supplied approximately 100 million pieces for this promotion alone.

Other than the popular small figures we associate with Wade, over the years they have also produced tea sets, nursery ware, tableware, tankards and souvenir items.

MARKS

Obviously, with so many 'Wade' companies on the go it is difficult to describe all of the marks associated with their production over the years. To further complicate matters, production records were only ever kept for 7 years, and many stamps would overlap in time periods. So it is very difficult to date pieces prior to the 1940's. It is possible to get a piece with 4 different stamps on the base!

The earliest stamps (1920's) feature the word 'ORCADIA' on the base, along with 'Wade Heath British made'. Wade Heath had some 20 different marks from 1928-1985; these can include the words Flaxman ware and Flaxman. George Wade had about 7 different marks, from the 1930's - 1950's. These were more simply 'Wade Made in England, Wade ovenproof etc. There are also marks stating Wade Ireland, from 1953-1980's onwards which would feature a shamrock as well and the words 'Irish porcelain', 'Shamrock pottery' and 'Celtic pottery'. These pieces are from the factory in Portadown, Northern Ireland that opened in 1946.

0018R&C Children's drum shaped toy box
£20 €28

0022R&C Collection of 1950's confectionery tins
£15 €21

0072R&C Collection of coloured vases
£15 - £30 €21 - €42

0085R&C Carved hardwood Elephant inlaid stool
£100 €140

0094R&C Collection of Devonware pottery
£5- £40 €7 - €56

0099R&C Mixture of Wedgewood plates & vases
£15 - £30 €21 - €42

Cheaper than Chips

834. Collection of coloured glass **£40 €56**

835. Bowl and cover **£50 €70**

839. Lladro figure of a girl and a chicken **£30 €42**

836. Liqueur decanter **£15 €21**

837. Pair Sitzendorf figures of gardeners **£80 €112**

838. Four Pendelphin figures **£35 €49**

840. Framed pot lid **£40 €56**

841. SylvaC, pottery rabbit **£30 €42**

842. Box Wade 'miniature' figures **£20 €28**

Pot Lids

Pot lids are thought to have come about around the 1850's and although there were many manufacturers, producing lids for jars of potted meats and savouries. Early manufacturers such as F&R Pratt are the most collectable. Decorated with transfer printed pictures on a variety of surfaces, of landscapes, portraits, and national events Valued at between £15 and £80 - well worth looking out for.

843. Royal Doulton 'Reflections' figure **£55** €**77**

845. Moorcroft tea cup and saucer **£105** €**147**

844. Quimper figure of the Virgin Mary and Child & repro staffs. figure of a Turk **£35 £15** €**49** €**21**

846. Breakfast cup and saucer **£10** €**14**

847. Silver plate tea pot, saucier and cream jug **£35** €**49**

848. Victorian mahogany brass bound stationary cabinet **£80** €**112**

849. Inside of picture 848.

LM32. Village collectibles 'Golf club' tea pot **£10** €**14**

851. Edwardian inlaid mahogany blue mantel clock **£80** €**112**

852. Pewter Liberty water jug with hinged cover **£80** €**112**

Cheaper than Chips

853. Brass bound tea box **£30 €42**

LM33. Wade 'fruit decoration' teapot **£15 €21**

855. Old radio **£20 €28**

857. Set scales **£20 €28**

856. Tiffany style lamp **£80 €112**

858. Repro water pump **£30 €42**

859. Box demijohns **£20 €28**

860. Umbrella & walking stick stand **£20 €28**

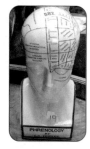

861. Phrenology head by I. Fowler **£25 €35**

862. Modern wall fountain, no pump **£10 €14**

863. 1960's Bush radio in white Bakelite **£20 €28**

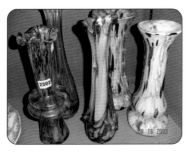

796. Five coloured glass vases **£25 €35**

797. Doulton part dinner and tea set **£60 €84**

802. Moorcroft vase **£160 €224**

798. Large qty Limoges **£150 €210**

799. Meissen comport **£45 €63**

800. Pair Dove candle sticks **£30 €42**

801. Tea set **£40 €56**

803. Royal Doulton figure 'Ellen' **£75 €105**

804. Base of picture 805.

Top Tips

It is impossible to predict what will appeal to collectors in the future. When you are looking to buy expensive items at carboot sales or auctions buy pieces you will love - they may be in your home for some time.

Cheaper than Chips

864. Old television and radio
£20 €28

865. Victorian cast iron
stove **£50 €70**

866. Two rabbit tureens,
two bird tureens
£30 €42

867. Three shoe lasts
£20 €28

868. Coca Cola set
£15 €21

869. Old telephone
£40 €56

870. Lorna Bailey vase & Royal
Doulton character jug 'North
American indian' **£45 £55 €63 €77**

871. Two pairs of scales and
weights **£30 €42**

872. Lorna Bailey jug and Bird
figure **£50 £22 €70 e31**

Coca-Cola

The American soft drink has been with us for virtually the whole of the 20th Century. And its exports have been shipped to the most remote islands and countries around the world. Although the bottle and content largely sold itself, items of memorabilia are collectable and collectors' clubs will pay handsomely for more sought after items. Worth collecting single pieces and building sets.

873. Wind-up gramophone
£80 €**112**

874. Toucan jug
£40 €**56**

875. Two boxes (one inside the other) **£50** €**70**

876. Framed plaque
£20 €**28**

877. Old telephone
£40 €**56**

878. Pair of continental vases **£20** €**28**

879. Crown Devon jug **£20** €**28**

880. Reproduction knife box
£50 €**70**

881. Gas mask
£10 €**14**

882. Dressing table set and tray **£20** €**28**

Cheaper than Chips

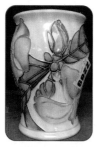

805. Moorcroft vase
£140 €196

806. Moorcroft vase
£195 €273

807. Base of picture 806.

808. Masons vase
£45 €63

810. Three blue pussy
cats **£20 €28**

811. Moorcroft vase
£180 €252

814. Wedgewood part dinner
and tea service **£50 €70**

812. Continental white and gilt dinner
and tea service **£40 €56**

809. Winstanley cat and Carlton ware
"Piggy" jug, pig's head money
box **£20 £50 €28 €70**

Top Tips

Whatever catches your eye at an auction or at a carboot sales - china, toys, tools, or furniture - always ensure the items you buy are well made. Quality sells now and will continue to do so in the future.

813. Ainsley cake plate and knife in box **£30 €42**

884. Samovar
£35 €49

883. Set of Wade 'piggy banks'
£200 €280

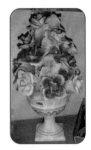

885. Posy pyramid
£15 €21

886. Coalport figure
£20 e28

888. Victorian leather ladies jewel box & ladies leather jewel box **£30 £25 €42 €35**

887. Early Bush television
£100 €140

889. Yamaha clarinet case
£100 €140

890. Inside of picture 889.

Cheaper than Chips

891. Boxed Pelham puppet
£30 €42

893. Old collection of toy trains
and rails **£80 €112**

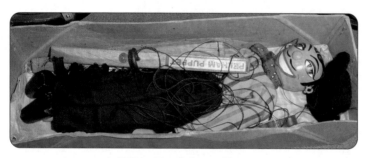

892. Inside of picture 891.

894. Turned wood boot jack
& copper warming pan
£30 each €42 each

895. Wall hanging perpetual
date calendar **£45 €63**

896. 19c. Lion mask, copper
fuel bin **£90 €126**

897. Brass trivet
£20 €28

Pelham Puppets

Makers of hand and string puppets popularly from the early 1950's. Pelham puppets in boxed and good condition can fetch up to £100. These often turn up at car boot sales and antique fairs, they made all types of novelty items, and most are collectable, but be on the look out for wooden limbs as these appear to be of most value.

898. Four piece egg
condiment
£40 **€56**

908. Bush radio
£25 **€35**

909. Continental figure
group **£15** **€21**

910. Poole Pottery
jug **£44** **€62**

911. Bottom of picture 910.

912. Set scales
£20 **€28**

913. Old clocking-in
machine **£50** **€70**

914. Victorian dome topped brass-banded
stationary box **£150** **€210** /Patent crystal
set **£80** **€112** / Biscuit tin **£25** **€35**

915. 19c. Ivory tusk and two
marine tusks **£35** **€49**

Cheaper than Chips

916. Copper plaque **£40** €56/
pair of Salter pocket balances and one level **£30** €42/
Slide preparation platform **£25** €35

917. Mamod steam engine
£100 €140

919. Scratch built
steam factory
£50 €70

920. Early 20c. Wicker picnic
hamper **£100** €140

922. Scratch built tin plate
railway engine **£50** €70

921. Walnut cased mantel
clock **£120** €168

923. Straw filled teddy
bear **£40** €56

924. Painted wooden
clock **£40** €56

925. Pair of gilt metal
figures on marble bases
(1 A/F) **£50** €70

918. Scratch built wooden tin plate railway engine **£60** €84

926. Carved walnut aneroid barometer **£170** €238

927. Collection of puppets **£50** €70

928. Two early vehicle lamps **£45** €63

929. Black lacquer gilt blue inkstand **£25** €35/ Decanter box and contents **£25** €35/ Ivory box and contents **£35** €49

930. Two copper kettles **£40** €56

931. Copper scuttle and brass trivet **£45** €63

932. Two brass folding spark guards and magazine rack **£50** €70

933. Copper samovar **£80** €112

934. Large oriental jar **£200** €280

935. Black leather case travel box and red box **£45** €63

Cheaper than Chips

899. Two chamber pots **£20 €28**

900. Desk lamp **£20 €28**

901. Globe drinks cabinet **£20 €28**

902. Old Bush Bakelite radio **£30 €42**

903. Set scale and weights **£5 €7**

905. Radiogram **£35 €49**

904. Moorland sugar box/cover **£30 €42**

906. Electrical testing set **£25 €35**

907. Inside of picture 906.

Bakelite

A resin discovered in the 1870's but only widely used in the 20th century. It was the most universally used of the early plastics.

Most people associate it with old radios and television sets, but virtually every house had more discrete items made from it such as light switches, plug sockets, dinner services or even jewellery.

Later hoovers and hundreds of other household items were made from it. As cast iron or steel became synonymous with the industrial revolution of the 1800's, Bakelite was second to none when it came to household items.

939. Continental Hors d'oeuvres dish £20 €28

936. 19c. Part tea set £50 €70

937. Jardiniere £20 €28

938. Box Armorial items £50 €70

940. Moorcroft candlestick £150 €210

941. 19c. Tea pot £30 €42

942. Pair of Satsuma vases £35 €49

943. Gaudy Welsh jug £30 €42

944. Garniture of three continental porcelain vases £100 €140

LM37. Wade 'Dressage' teapot £15 €21

Cheaper than Chips

946. Doulton Lambeth salt glazed stoneware item **£60 €84**

947. Pewter water or wine ewer **£40 €56**

948. Etched glass decanter **£25 €35**

949. Two Carlton ware boxes and covers **£50 €70**

950. Painted blue glass ewer **£20 €28**

951. Three blue and white transfer printed plates **£15 €21**

952. Pottery dish **£20 €28**

953. Mason's Ironstone plate and continental plaque **£35 €49**

954. Enoch Wedgewood part dessert set **£32 €45**

Majolica...

...is the name given to a type of earthenware introduced in 1851 by Minton. These wares were richly modelled, and then dipped in tin-enamel glaze, and highly decorated. Because of the strength, and durability of the finished glaze, many other household items came into use, such as sewer pipes, tiles, and cooking items. Although today we mainly associate Majolica with heavily embossed pottery.

955. Majolica jug
£80 €112

LM38. Big wheel
teapot
£7 €10

957. Pair of Kutani
vases **£80 €112**

958. Salt glazed
stoneware jug
£40 €56

960. Cut glass decanter,
stopper & celery
glass **£50 €70**

959. Continental porcelain vase
and Poole Pottery vase
£20 €28 £50 €70

961. Continental
figure **£5 €7**

962. Sugar box and cover
and pair of plates
£20 €28

LM39. Tom & Jerry figures
£20 €28

964. Devon ware tea pots
£100 €140

Cheaper than Chips

786. Masons hydra jug
£45 €63

787. Crown Devon cress dish
and stand **£30 €42**

788. Six Wedgewood blue
Jasper ware **£35 €49**

789. Royal Doulton Grantham
pattern charger **£30 €42**

790. Art Deco style
coffee set **£30 €42**

791. Cantonese vase and
rice dish cover stands and
spoon **£35 €49**

LM29. Royal Doulton figure
of the year 1997 'Jessica'
£150 €210

793. Clarice Cliff vase
£80 €112

794. Painted pink glasses, vase
and cover **£50 €70**

China

When buying items of China such as figures, plates or crockery it is important to check that it is in perfect condition. Damage can devalue an item by more than 50%.

795. Three graduated Bisto meat dishes **£50 €70**

965. Moorland Leopard sugar box and cover **£45 €63**

966. Qty. Wedgewood Jasper ware items **£60 €84**

970. Hand painted plate **£30 €42**

968. Meissen tea pot **£50 €70**

LM40. China Camel **£10 €14**

967. Continental tramp figure **£25 €35**

972. Booths part dinner service **£50 €70**

973. Booths part dinner service with pictures 972 and 974.

974. Booths part dinner service with pictures 972 and 973

Cheaper than Chips

971. Decanter and six glasses **£35 €49**

975. Pair of continental vases **£250 €350**

976. Copeland Spode jug **£30 €42**

977. Two swan posies **£15 €21**

978. Qty. Wedgewood Jasper ware items **£40 €56**

979. Italian sauce tureen and cover with ladle **£60 €84**

980. Three Poole Pottery items **£25 €35**

981. Three flying toucans **£48 €67**

Copeland & Spode

Founded in 1833 by W.T. Copeland & Garret; when the pair took over Spode factory the name changed to Copeland Late Spode, then Copeland, but today it is known as Spode. They produced mainly fine porcelain pieces for the table, produced in a high glaze finish and quickly became very popular with Victorians, and indeed collectors today, as even single items are both attractive and very collectable. Look out for fine examples of cream or milk jugs and fine table ware.

982. Pair Gien tankards
£60 €83

983. Qty. Armorial items
£70 €98

984. Three oriental flower
bricks **£40 €56**

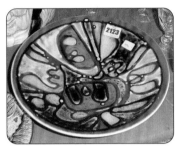

985. Poole Pottery dish
£60 €84

986. Continental Majolica
plate **£30 €42**

LM41. Twins ice boy & girl
£70 €98

988. Pair of blue glass
vases **£30 €42**

989. Doulton Lambeth
salt glazed stoneware-
hunting jug **£40 €56**

991. Child's part tea set
£40 €56

Cheaper than Chips

698. Carved horse head
£50 €70

699. Tin-plated bus
£45 €63

701. Tin plate toy
£28 €39

700. Tin plate locomotive
£25 €35

702. Set scales & weights
£20 €28

703. Art Deco clock
£35 €49

704. Copper kettle and
trivet **£30 €42**

705. Three flying Toucans
£48 €67

Games

The best advice for buying games is not to buy incomplete sets. A couple of missing pieces can dramatically effect the price. This does not however apply to all incomplete sets, Train sets and Meccano if incomplete can be added to or broken up to complete other sets, thus enhancing their value.

992. Two shire horses figures **£30** €**42**

993. Royal Doulton character jug 'Blacksmith' **£50** €**70**

994. Blue and white serving dish **£50** €**70**

LM42. Heart shaped Lady Diana & Charles box & cover **£10** €**14**

996. Pair of blue and white oriental vases **£50** €**70**

997. Pair of staffs figures **£80** €**112**

998. Lorna Bailey jug **£50** €**70**

999. Qty. Wedgewood blue and white Jasper ware **£40** €**56**

1000. Continental centrepiece **£50** €**70**

1001. Devil Tobacco jar **£50** €**70**

Cheaper than Chips

1002. Collection of continental figures **£30 €42**

1003. Pair of figures and figure group **£30 €42**

1004. Two Honiton potteries items **£50 €70**

1005. Two Tiger figures **£20 €28**

1006. Sabine glass vase **£80 €112**

1008. Ornate brass fire fender **£100 €140**

1007. Oriental figure of a Japanese woman **£30 €42**

1009. Pair of branch candelabrum on marble **£45 €63**

1010. Smiths alarm clock **£25 €35**

1016. Two carved wooden elephants **£40** €**56**

1012. Copper plaque **£40** €**56**

1013. Patinated metal figure: Women and two children **£70** €**98**

1014. Patent crystal set **£85** €**119**

1011. Patinated bronze figure **£50** €**70**

1015. World War II biscuit tin **£20** €**28**

1017. Oriental cast and china table lamp **£100** €**140**

1018. Victorian brass kettle on stand with burner **£45** €**63**

1019. George VI coronation mug **£30** €**42**

LM43. Royal Worcester flower posy **£20** €**28**

LM46. Wedgewood & Co. Scottie in basket **£10** €**14**

LM47. Country bird collection Great spotted woodpecker **£5** €**7**

Cheaper than Chips

122. Oriental bronze Hindu figure
£45 €**63**

123, Stuffed teddy & pussy cat
£30 €**42**

124. Fireside companion set
£25 €**35**

125. Brass fireside log box
£40 €**56**

126. 2 brass spark guards
£40 €**56**

127. 19c copper coal scuttle and shovel **£60** €**85**

128. 19c Oriental blue & white jardiniere **£80** €**112**

129. Brass coal scuttle
£40 €**56**

130. Barometer
£30 €**42**

Top Tips

Fireside brass or copper boxes, now virtually redundant in today's homes, are still popular among collectors. These items are most popular with people who want to enhance period character around original fireplaces. Most auctions and carboot sales have a good collection of items for sale.

1023. Bisque figure
£40 €56

1024. Ruby and gilt glass beaker and Bristol green glass **£25 €35 each**

1025. Poole Pottery bird figures **£40 €56 each**

1026. Goebel fire mug and dog figure **£40 €56 £10 €14**

LM48. Goldfinch **£5 €7**

1028. Beswick owl **£40 €56**

LM49. The Little Owl **£5 €7**

1029. Chinese oval spoon tray **£40 €56**

1030. Staffordshire figure group **£100 €140**

1032. Pair of continental figures cherubs and birds **£50 €70**

Cheaper than Chips

1033. Lladro figure of a golfer
£60 €84

1035. Wade piggy and Staffordshire figure
£30 £40 €42 €56

1036. Moorcroft jug
£190 €266

1037. Beswick fox gentleman
£35 €49

1034. Lorna Bailey salt and pepper
£50 €70

1038. Pewter coffee pot
£20 €28

1039. Silver plate claret jug & sugar caster
£45 €63

1040. Six-bottle condiment set
£70 €98

1041. Four piece silver plated tea set
£40 €56

1042. Hotel ware tea service on tray **£30** €42

1043. Half lobed coffee service **£30** €42

Silver Plate...

...is the one item that I tend to steer well clear of at any sale unless it is of an unusual design, or some other endearing factor. It's fine if you particularly like the piece but as a collectable that may increase in value or use then avoid them. Look out for solid silver instead, it will always give you some return, and be more collectable.

1045. Fireside knight tool rest
£70 €98

1044. Three piece plated tea service **£30 €42**

1046. Box of continental cheese dishes
£50 €70

1047. Vase
£15 €21

1048. Moorland tea pot **£45 €63**

1049. Walnut wall clock
£35 €49

1050. Pair of vases
£15 €21

1051. Barometer
£40 €56

1052. Two Wade pigs
£40 €56

1053. Pair of transfer printed vases
£15 €21

Cheaper than Chips

131. Teddy Bear
£30 €42

132. Polly portable phonograph
£100 €140

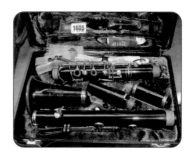

133. Clarinet in case
£70 €98

134. Ship's bell "Kelpie"
£45 €63

135. Baby composite dolly
£50 €70

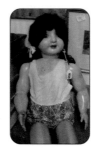

136. Large composite dolly
£100 €140

139. 2 cut glass decanters and stoppers £40 €56

138. Indian double bladed hunting knife £40 €56

137. Teddy bear circa 1950's £60 €85

Composition Dollies...

...is the phrase given to dolls when they are assembled from separate components made from different materials. For example china or plastic heads together with fabric bodies. These items vary greatly in value and are often not marked. It is worth checking aged dolls prior to selling as top manufacturers can collect thousands of pounds. Please see picture 135 and 136.

1054. Pair of cast figures
£15 €21

1055. Pair of Moorland items, tea and milk jug **£70 €98**

1056. Set Moorland tea service
£90 €126

1057. Art deco figure
£50 €70

1058. Art deco figure
£40 €56

1059. Part liqueur set painted glass
£20 €28

1060. Poole Pottery vase
£40 €56

1061. Base of picture of 1060.

1062. Oak mantel clock
£25 €35

1063. Cast metal figure
£30 €42

1064. Moorland service tea set and mugs
£120 €168

Cheaper than Chips

1065. Cast metal figure dog and pheasant **£40 €56**

1066. Cast figure, cockerel and lizard **£40 €56**

1067. Box china animal figures **£30 €42**

1068. Pair of plated candlesticks **£20 €28**

1069. Moorland sugar caster **£40 €56**

LM50. The Jay **£5 €7**

1071. Cast Red Indian and eagle figure **£30 €42**

1072. Three glass photo frames **£30 €42**

1073. Two cheese covers **£30 €42**

Cheaper than Chips

Top Tips

Shelley includes a large range of items made from the Foley China Factories and then from 1925 onwards by Wileman and Company. Look out for dishes, vases, plates and tea sets. Please see picture 146.

142. Pair Persian candle sticks **£40** **€56**

140. Green glass bowl **£20** **€28**

141. Pair Chinese ginger vases
£35 **€49**

143. Continental figure of a
hunting dog **£30** **€42**

144. Tureen & cover
£90 **€126**

145. Set 6 Copeland Spode
plates **£50** **€70**

146. Shelley bowl
£35 **€49**

147. Picture. Base of pic.146

Cheaper than Chips

1074. Pair of
foot bellows
£20 €28

1075. Brass jardiniere
£18 €25

1076. Wind up
gramophone
£80 €112

1077. Toocan figure
lamp **£40 €56**

1078. Continental pot and
cover **£10 €14**

1079. Oak cased
wall clock
£40 €56

1080. Wade liquor barrels
£40 €56

1081. Tin plate
robot
£20 €28

1082. Tin plate
circus elephant
£20 €28

1083. Lorna Bailey jug
£50 €70

1084. China figure
group **£20 €28**

Tin Plate Robots...

...have been around since the early 1930's and were mainly clock work models, but with the introduction in the 40's and 50's of battery power and remote control they became quite sophisticated. And it's partly this reason why they have become so collectable today. Although there are many out there to start collecting, pay particular attention to damage as this will greatly effect the value. Boxed and in good condition early robots can fetch up to £1000.

1085. Model steam roller cart **£35 €49**

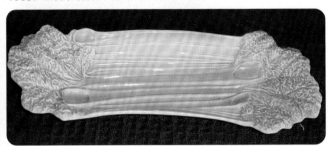

LM44. Royal Winton celery dish
£20 €28

LM51. Barn owl
£5 €7

LM52. Blue tit
£5 €7

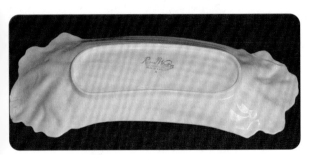

LM45. Base of picture LM44.

1090. Guitar and banjo
£20 €28 each

1091. Part dressing
table set **£30 €42**

1092. China wall clock
£35 €49

1093. 1950's radio
£25 €35

1094. 'Safe' tea pot
£20 €28

Cheaper than Chips

148. Bowl & vase
£15 €21

149. Continental vase with cupids £45 €63

150. 4 painted plates
£40 €56

152. Decanter & stopper
£25 €35

151. Ashworth brothers part dinner service £70 €98

153. Doulton Lambeth stoneware jug
£40 €56

154. Picture of base pic.153

155. A Whitefrairs glass vase £25 €35

156. 19c. Chinese ginger jar £35 €49

157. Salt glazed stoneware jug
£40 €56

Top Tips

Whitefriars Glass was founded in London in the 17th Century, producing traditional hand blown items. These included vases, bowls, windows and paperweights. They are still in production today, look out for paperweights, revived versions of venetian glass forms and lead cut crystal.

1095. Toy box tea pot
£25 €**35**

1096. Metal figure
cast goat
£35 €**49**

1097. Metal figure cast pheasant
£30 €**42**

1098. Pair brass bellows
£25 €**35**

1099. Willow pattern
meat dish **£15** €**21**

1100. Violin in case, intact
£35 €**49**

1101. Seven
ceramic tiles
£80 €**112**

1104. Stoneware
oil lamp
£50 €**70**

1102. Four Dalmatian
dog napkin holders
£25 €**35**

1103. Brass pen tray etc. **£25** €**35**

Cheaper than Chips

1105. Deco copper kettle
£65 €90

1106. Mahogany and brass cigar cutter
£30 €42

1107. Pair brass candlesticks
£35 €49

1108. Victorian blue glass and gilt candlestick
£60 €84

1109. Two Bakelite cigarette dispensers
£40 €56

1110. Two walnut inkstands
£120 €168

1112. Cast metal figure
£30 €42

1113. Walnut cased mantel clock
£200 €280

1114. Ice cream bombe £30 €42

1115. Burrwood needlework box
£90 €126

1116. Oriental enamel vase damaged
£50 €70

Art Deco

Art Deco takes its name from the Paris Exposition Internationale des Arts Decoratifs of 1925. And fashion designers of the 1920's & 30's soon picked up on the style of its soft lines and warm colours - which made it just as suitable for furniture and building design to the dramatic, abstract and angular shapes that adorn many thousands of items today - from figurines to perfume bottles, and countless household items.

Cheaper than Chips

Top Tips

Cranberry Glass is another coloured glass popular with Victorians from light shades to bowls and dishes. Please see picture 162.

158. Minton part coffee set
£30 €42

159. Moorcroft dish **£100** €140

160. Crown Staffordshire coffee set **£40** €56

161. Wedgewood sauce tureen & cover **£30** €42

162. American cranberry rose bowl & vase
£40 €56 **each**

163. Shelly tea set
£60 €84

164. Masons ironstone dish **£25** €35

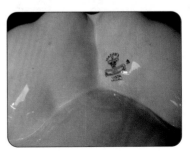

165. Base of pic 164

Cheaper than Chips

1117. Brass warming pan **£40 €56**

1119. Teddy bear **£65 €91**

1120. Quart pewter tankard **£35 €49**

1121. Seven jelly and aspic moulds **£80 €112**

1123. Painted Victorian mantle clock **£25 €35**

1124. Early 19c. Oak cutlery tray **£80 €112**

1128. Copper coal scuttle **£45 €63**

1122. Brass domed perpetual mantel clock **£70 €98**

1125. Oak mantel clock **£25 €35**

1126. Smiths electric mantel clock **£45 €63**

1127. Medieval knights metal helmet **£80 €112**

Cheaper than Chips

1118. Black lacquered papier mâché box **£60 €84**

1129. 19c. Cast iron fireplace guard **£100 €140**

1131. Bayonet in sheath and Oriental steel knife **£40 €56 each**

1130. Collection of World War 1 memorabilia **£70 €98**

1132. 19c. Walnut toilet mirror **£60 €84**

1133. Indian copper and brass plaque **£40 €56**

1134. Metal figure 'The Dandy' **£200 €280**

1135. Regency walnut swing mirror **£90 €126**

1136. Moorcroft vase **£190 €266**

1137. Kutani vase **£50 €70**

1138. Continental coffee set on tray **£130 €182**

Cheaper than Chips

1139. Moorcroft vase
£130 €182

1140. Moorcroft
vase
£200 €280

1141. Biscuit barrel and
Mason's jar with cover
£35 €49

LM53. The swallow
£5 €7

1143. Iridescent glass bowl
£35 €49

1144. Poole Pottery vase
£40 €56

1145. Royal Crown Derby
tea set **£130 €182**

1146. Box Armorial
ware **£70 €98**

1147. Two ships in bottles
£25 a pair €35 a pair

1148. Hand painted
pink glass vases
£60 €84 a pair

166. Ainsley Strawberry &
Cream set **£30** €**42**

167. Green glass decanter
& label **£60** €**85**

168. Victorian comport
£35 €**49**

169. Clarice Cliff collector's mask
"Wedgewood" **£50** €**70**

170. Blue & white willow pattern
meat dish **£40** €**56**

171. Chinese blue glazed
Duck **£70** €**98**

172. Royal Worcester jar &
cover **£60** €**84**

173. Continental figure
group **£40** €**56**

174. Pair Vases
£70 €**98**

175. Victorian commemorative
plate **£25** €**35**

Cheaper than Chips

176. Pair Dr Syntax plates **£40** €56

177. Quantity glass ware **£30** €42

178. Couples teaset on tray **£70** €98

179. Modern monkey ornament **£20** €28

180. Kutani charger **£100** €140

181. Base of pic 180.

182. Three Wedgewood items **£25** €35

183. 2 Midwinter plates & Cornishware sugar sifter **£40** €56

184. Decanter & stopper **£30** €42

Top Tips

Wedgwood is best known for decorated vases, bowls and dishes with a low relief pattern on a light blue background. However before these designs became popular most Wedgwood items for domestic use where quite plain with a matte glaze. Look out for anything by Keith Murray from 1933 onwards.

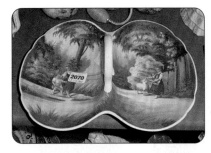

1160. Hors d'œuvres
dish **£35** €**49**

1150. Royal Copenhagen
bottle vase
£35 €**49**

1151. Collection of
pharmaceutical
glass **£35** €**49**

1155. Ruby pickle
and glass vase
£45 €**63**

LM54. Nut thatch
£5 €**7**

1153. Continental
figure group
£50 €**70**

1154. Five Japanese
china items
£30 €**42**

LM55. Song thrush
£5 €**7**

LM56. Blackbird
£5 €**7**

1158. Hermes original ashtray
£35 €**49**

1159. Goldscheider
figure
£60 €**84**

Cheaper than Chips

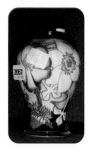

1149. Moorcroft vase **£150 €210**

1161. Pair of candlesticks and table centre display **£40 €56**

1162. Commemorative tea pot **£20 €28**

1164. Pair of oriental vases **£40 €56**

1163. Selection of cream ware items **£30 €42**

LM57. Nightingale **£5 €7**

1166. Opaque glass and gilt vase **£40 €56**

LM58. Longtailed tit **£5 €7**

1168. Ainsley tea service **£200 e280**

LM59. House sparrow **£5 €7**

1170. Part Royal Worcester dinner service **£40 €56**

Buyer's Premium

The auction house can rarely lose money on the items they sell, as they charge both the seller and the buyer without exception.

Buyer's premium at most auction houses is 15 - 20% and for sellers it is usually per lot or item.

LM60. Blue & white tureen & ladle
£15 €21

1172. Bretby jug
£35 €49

1173. Two cut glass wine tumblers
£20 €28

1174. Ruby glass vase and a Stoneware vase
£20 €28 each

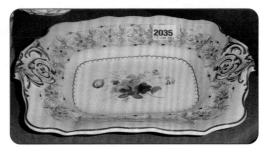

1175. Copeland serving dish **£40 €56**

1176. Staffordshire figure group
£35 €49

1177. Three Whitefriars vases **£35 €49**

1178. Green Majolica leaf dish & plates
£25 €35

1179. Crackle glass flask & commemorative plate **£35 €49**

Cheaper than Chips

1180. Sargamine Majolica jug **£90** €126

1181. Capo Di Monte fig group **£150** €210

1182. Commemorative tankard **£15** €21

1183. Studio glass vase **£20** €28

1184. Mason's Ironstone bowl **£25** €35

1185. Two cut glass decanters & stoppers **£35** €49

1186. Samson bowl **£55** €77

1187. Three framed Pratware pot lids **£100** €140

1188. Late Victorian walnut Vienna wall clock **£220** €308

1189. Victorian rocking horse **£120** €168

1190. Lustred slop pail & cover **£50** €70

Capodimonte

Produced in Spain from 1759 to the present day Capodimonte has a large following around the world. Famous for its fine porcelain or paste figures. Early examples run into thousands of pounds. Massed produced pieces of the 20th Century are obviously nowhere near as valuable, but still have a place in the heart for the nostalgic collector. Look to pay upwards of £100 for nice 20th century pieces.

1191. Victorian painted mirror/candle holder
£85 €**119**

1192. Selection silver plated cruets on tray **£35** €**49**

1193. Silver on copper bottle coaster
£30 €**42**

1194. Silver plate Claret jug, tea box and sugar caster
£35 €**49**

1195. Pewter coffee pot
£40 €**56**

1196. Plate teapot
£20 €**28**

1197. 6 Bottle condiment set
£45 €**63**

1198. Selection silver plated tankards **£25** €**35**

1199. Solid silver 3 piece tea service
£270 €**378**

1200. Plated domed top meat cover
£65 €**91**

Cheaper than Chips

1201. Selection silver plate fish knives
£20 €28

1202. Entrée dish and cover, silver plate **£25 €35**

LM62. QEII Silver jubilee cup
£5 €7

LM63. King Edward V1 coronation cup
£10 €14

LM64. Reverse of picture LM63.

1207. Set of wine glasses
£30 €42

LM61. Tureen & ladle
£15 €21

LM65. John Paul II 1982 commemorative mug
£5 €7

1209. 4 Parian ware figures and jugs
£85 €119

1210. Staffordshire figure **£35** €**49**

542. Silver plated meat cover **£50** €**70**

543. Three piece silver tea set **£150** €**210**

544. Pair of silver plated candlesticks with snuffers **£60 each** €**84 each**

545. Silver plated four egg cruet with spoons **£45** €**63**

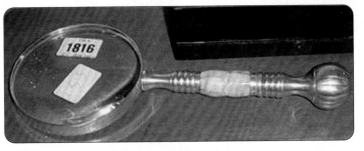

546. Magnifying glass **£10** €**14**

547. Silver salt and pepper cruet in box **£30** €**42**

548. Two silver plated trays **£50** €**70**

549. Tea pot, plated milk jug, sugar bowl **£25** €**35**

Cheaper than Chips

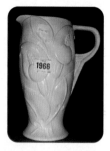

185. Staffordshire jug
£25 €35

186. Poole pottery vase
£40 €56

187. Picture of base of 186.

188. Set of 3 graduated Doulton Burslem jugs **£160** €224

189. Royal Doulton Punch & Judy
£60 €84

190. Base of pic. 189

191. Tuscan china tea set
£70 €98

192. Two Liliput Lane cottages **£30** €42

193. Two cut glass Decanters & stoppers **£50** €70

Staffordshire Pottery...

... founded in the late 17th Century produced virtually every sort of household item. Most notable designers are the Elers Brothers and Thomas Tofts. Staffordshire animal figures were produced in huge numbers during the Victorian era, as were figurines of famous people such as Queen Victoria and Napoleon. The area around Stoke on Trent is still known as The Potteries.

194. Swedish studio glass paperweight **£50 €70**

1211. Millefiori paperweight **£25 €35**

1212. A Russian Koush **£55 €77**

LM66. QEII Silver jubilee mug **£5 €7**

1214. Small Moorcroft dish **£40 €56**

1215. Two Belique preserve pots **£65 €91**

1216. Miniature Moorcroft vase **£80 €112**

LM67. Charles & Diana wedding mug **£5 €7**

1218. Satsuma teapot, cup, saucer & plate **£85 €119**

1219. Moorcroft vase **£160 €224**

LM68. Royal Worcester tea-cup **£5 €7**

Cheaper than Chips

1220. Pair Majolica leaf dishes
£55 €77

1222. Pair Samson sheep &
Staffordshire sheep
£40 + £30 €56 + €42

1223. Kutani vase
£55 €77

1225. Samovar
£65 €91

1226. Metal jar
& cover
£45 €63

1227. Japanese musical
jewellery box **£20 e28**

1228. Moorland jug &
Lorna Bailey salt/pepper
£30 €42   £40 €56

1229. Poole Pottery
vase **£55 €77**

1230. Base of pic 1229.

Samovar

The Samovar is a 19th Century invention for boiling water in the new and upcoming Victorian tea rooms. Although its origins are thought to be Russian probably because of its name, there are many different designs out there today, and surprisingly in good supply. Usually made from copper or brass, or a mix of both, they can be highly decorated or moulded, they are not recommended for practical use, purely decorative.

1224. Pair Rockingham plates
£40 €**56**

195. Royal Doulton figure Coralie **£90** €**126**

196. Base of pic 195.

197. Myott & son jug **£38** €**53**

198. Base of pic 197.

199. Two Hydra jugs **£40** €**56**

200. Royal Doulton jug Athos **£55** €**77**

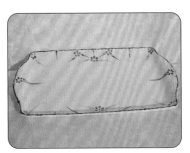

HY42. Grindley sweet or fruit tray **£10** €**14**

202. Cluck Cluck decanter **£30** €**42**

203. Two blue glass jugs & plates **£50** €**70**

Cheaper than Chips

204. Copeland Spode toilet set **£160** €**224**

205. Cantonese cake stand
with ormolu mounts
£20 €**28**

206. Caithness
Moonflower
paperweight **£20** €**28**

207. Minton part tea set
£45 €**63**

209. Silver-plated oval tray &
other items **£45** €**63**

210. 3 piece silver service
on tray **£80** €**112**

208. Baluster water jug
£20 €**28**

211. Muffins dish & cover
£50 €**70**

212. Silver plate tea
pot **£30** €**42**

Caithness Glass

Caithness Glass' Moonflower is shown in picture 206. Look out for first issues depicting Mercury, Mars, Saturn and Venus from 1969.

This limited edition set of four was sold for around £45, today they are valued at between £1,700 and £1,900.

213. Leather bound flask with tots **£40 e56**

1231. Leopard pot & cover **£35 €49**

1232. Chelsea Burslem mug **£30 €42**

1233. Base of pic 1232.

1234. Childs part tea service **£45 €63**

1235. Fairy bowl **£35 €49**

1236. 3 tier cake stand **£35 €49**

1237. Lorna Bailey jug **£50 €70**

1238. Boots inhaler **£20 €28**

1239. Royal Corona chamber pot **£30 €42**

Cheaper than Chips

LM71. Transfer printed 'Hydra' jug
£10 €14

1241. Set continental figures
£15 €21

1242. Worcester casserole dish **£15** €21

1243. German stoneware jug
£30 €42

1244. Cast figure of cat
£20 €28

1245. Pair oriental vases **£20** €28

1246. Moorland jug
£35 €49

1247. Box woodworking planes **£20** €28

1248. 35mm camera with attachments boxed
£30 €42

Cast Figures

This is an area for the specialist collector really. You will find quite a few examples of cast figures around at any car-boot sale or antique fair, and unless you know what you are looking for, or particularly like a piece then 'buyer beware', unless signed or by a well know sculptor, these pieces are usually quite well marked up. Sporting figures can bring the best return.

1249. Pair of chargers
£20 €28

1250. Three horse brass
martingales
£25 €35

1251. Pair gold plated
bath taps
£25 €35

1252. Pair brass
candlesticks
£15 €21

1253. Metal cast
figure of goat
£45 €63

1254. Oak case clock
£35 €49

1255. Glass jug
£10 €14

1256. Brass desk stand
£20 €28

1257. Dutch lemonade set
£20 €28

1258. Metal racing figure
group £80 €112

Cheaper than Chips

214. Victorian silver plate tea pot **£30 €42**

216. Ironstone hydra jug **£50 €70**

217. Royal Doulton figure Sharon **£100 €140**

215. Silver plate magnifying glass **£30 €42**

218. Pair continental scent bottles **£90 €140**

219. Royal Doulton figure **£90 €140**

220. Coalport chalice **£100 €140**

221. Set 6 Copeland Spode egg cups **£50 €70**

222. Moorcroft vase **£150 €210**

Top Tips

Copeland Spode (featured in picture 221) was founded by W. Copeland and Garrett in 1833. Today it is known as Spode, which is the name carried before the two took over the Staffordshire Pottery from Josiah Spode who establishes the company as far back as 1770. Early works included fine stoneware, creamware and the introduction of transfer printed items.

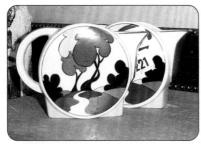

1259. 2 Moorland jugs
£45 €63

LM69. Royal Vienna urn on stand
£30 €42

1261. Lustre bowl & bread plate
£25 €35

1262. Copper bed pan
£45 €63

1263. Collection blue glass vases & bells
£20 €28

1264. Lorna Bailey jug £40 €56

1265. Art deco style mirror £40 €56

1266. Toucan figure
£30 €42

1267. Table centre piece
£35 €49

1268. Wade toucan jug
£45 €63

1269. 6 Roemer glasses
£20 €28

LM70. Reverse of Royal Vienna urn pic LM69.

Cheaper than Chips

1271. Biscuit barrel
£10 €14

1272. Oriental jardinière
£20 €28

1273. Pair plated
candlesticks
£15 €21

1274. Wade biscuit barrel
& mug **£35 €49**

1275. Pair Poole Pottery dolphins
£30 €42

1276. Dolls house in
edwardian style
£200 €280

1277. Moorland 3 piece tea set
£55 €77

1278. Continental
jardiniere **£20 €28**

1279. Coronation mug & plates
George VI **£30 €42**

1280. Modern guitar
£45 €63

223. Japanese bowl & cover **£40** €**56**

Cheaper than Chips

SylvaC, from the early part of the 20th Century has produced some very popular collectable items. Due to mass production of these typically green and brown china items, they are relatively inexpensive. Most 1950's and 1960's homes had celery jugs, wall pockets or woodland scenes in SylvaC and although it is still produced, some 1930's and 1940's are becoming quite valuable.

224. Continental porcelain cream sugar set **£40** €**56**

226. Six star cut Champagne glasses **£70** €**98**

225. Wedgewood pot & cover **£30** €**42**

227. Continental porcelain box **£80** €**112**

228. Three porcelain boxes & scent bottle **£30** €**42**

229. Sylvac Bunny **£40** €**56**

230. Commemorative Victorian jubilee jug **£40** €**56**

231. Royal Doulton limited edition Bell **£25** €**35**

232. Royal Doulton figure **£40** €**56**

Masons Patent Ironstone China - History

In 1804 Miles Mason set up a factory near Newcastle Under Lyme, to produce the porcelain he called 'semi-china'. At first the quality was not appreciated, but in 1813 Charles James Mason took out a patent for 'Patent Ironstone China' and with the added ingredient of china it became more desirable. The pieces had a much finer quality and were tastefully designed with a Chinese influence. Most examples are tea ware, dessert and dinner services, toilet sets and breakfast sets, in fact nearly all of the products were of a 'useable nature' with less than 1% being decorative.

Tablewares were produced specifically for auction around the country and the company flooded the market with many faulty pieces being sold. These faults, known about at factory stage as the tears or cracks in the pottery had often been glazed over.

Due to flooding the market in this way and not setting up any retail stockists, the durability of the products and decline in popularity of Chinese designs, it lead to the eventual bankruptcy of the company in 1848.

Many of the moulds were sold to Francis Morley and the name Morley was added under the Masons former standard crown mark.

In 1858 Morley went into partnership with Ashworth & Bros. LTD to become GL Ashworth & Bros. LTD. This name continued until its change in 1968 to Masons Ironstone China Ltd.

Ashworth re-issued Masons original shapes and patterns and it is difficult to tell the difference. Even so some of the re-issues can be valuable antiques as well. The main difference is in the body of the piece; the re-issues are not as compact or heavy as the originals. The underglaze blue parts of design are of a lighter tint then the dark blue original. Over the 100 years that Ashworth has been producing, the number one pattern has been the 'grasshopper design', now called regency or regency ducks.

PRODUCTS

Dinner services sold for their durability. They mainly featured Chinese landscapes and willow pattern designs. They were richly patterned in red blue green and gold, with bold areas of red, rich dark under glaze and 'mazarine' blue.

The dessert services and breakfast sets were decorated in much the same way. There were also fire places or mantels, from miniature models 12" high to 6ft wide, marked with a pre-Victorian royal arms with wording 'China Chimney piece. Mason and Co. Patentees Staffordshire potteries, not visible if built into a wall. There were a minimal amount of flowerpots, vases and jugs along with sundials and toilet seats.

COLLECTING

Complete services are worth more, and on the very rare side are pieces made to special order with regimental arms etc. on them.

There are a number of 'similar' types of pottery around, pieces marked 'Turners Patent', from around 1800, mainly painted with Chinese and English views. Spode, has similar earthenware pieces, it is difficult to date the introduction of these sets. It was called 'stone china' and later 'new stone china'. Their main rival was Davenport.

There are other manufacturers around in the early 1800's, with no marks on their pieces.

MARKS

The first pieces were rarely marked, occasionally having M. Mason. Cups and saucers (smaller items) were never marked.

1800-1813, sometimes see 'semi china warranted' on larger pieces. Sometimes pattern numbers 1-100 before 1805. (the Ashworth re-issues of these pieces have impressed numerals to indicate date - month number and last 2 digits of year of manufacture).

In 1813 many different sets of initials were in use for example G & CJM, GM & CJ Mason.

After 1813 ' Patent Ironstone China' in a circle, was used on one or two of the larger pieces in a set.

In 1825 'Fenton Stoneworks' or 'Delph Lane' appear, then from 1826-1845 the marks incorporate 'granite china' and Masons Bandana ware'.

After 1848 the mark becomes Ashworths.

Cheaper than Chips

1281. Set kitchen scales & weights £35 €49

1282. Boxed canteen cutlery £35 €49

1283. Open box of picture 1282.

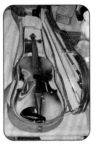

1284. Cased violin £40 €56

1285. Hand powered fire alarm bell £25 €35

1286. Pair hardwood twist candlesticks £15 €21

1287. Mason's Ironstone bowl & saucers £15 €21

1288. Moorland plate £30 €42

1289. Cast metal photo frames £30 €42

1290. Brass fire fender £20 €28

Cheaper than Chips

1291. 3 Drums
£20 €28

1292. Electric one-armed bandit
£85 €120

1293. Oriental wood figure of a dragon
£80 €112

1294. 2 Modern cast fountain masks
£20 €28

1295. 1990's fruit machine
£70 €98

1296. Guitar
£20 €28

1297. Guitar
£20 €28

1298. Brass table top & stand £35 €49

1299. Needlework fire screen
£30 €42

1300. Two hanging outside candle lights
£20 €28

1301. Oak cased wall clock
£35 €49

1302. Set tea cards framed
£15 €21

Cheaper than Chips

1303. Two transfer
printed potties
£30 €42

1304. Collection reproduction
glass bottles **£30 €42**

1305. Slipper bed pan
£10 €14

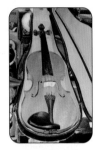

1306. Violin in case
£35 €49

1307. 1950's
Pin ball table
£85 €119

1308. Part dressing table set
£15 €21

1309. Copper
coal/log bucket
£30 €42

1310. Pottery
goblets & jar
£10 €14

1311. Brass trumpet in box
£20 €28

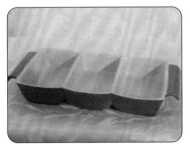

HY03. Poole pottery
segment dish
£10 €14

Cheaper than Chips

1313. Royal Doulton figure 'Christine' **£80** €112

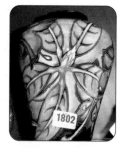

1314. Moorcroft vase **£300** €420

1315. Moorcroft vase **£145** €203

1316. Base of pic 1315.

HY04. Louatts Langley ware milk jug **£10** €14

HY05. Charles & Diana commemorative plate **£12** €17

HY06. Pair of Crown Trent cups, blackberry pattern. **£5** €7

1319. Royal Doulton vase **£45** €63

1320. Doulton Lambeth toby jug **£50** €70

1321. Doulton Lambeth saltglazed stoneware mug **£40** €56

1322. Wade novelty teapot **£30** €42

1324. Royal Doulton miniature character jugs **£100** €140

Salt Glaze...

...was produced by adding common salt into a kiln at a certain temperature; this then vaporised to a soda to give the appearance of a dull-pitted orange colour to the finish. Mainly use for storage jars tiles and pipes by the Victorians.

It was commonly used by many potters through the 19th Century particularly, Royal Doulton and The Martin Brothers. And more commonly used pots and tankards began to appear, the process was abandoned by many though as it was thought to be dangerous.

242. Small Moorcroft
dish **£60** €**84**

233. Moorcroft bowl
£90 €**126**

234. Base of picture 233.

235. Two blue & white
vases **£40** €**56**

236. Five Wade items
£40 €**56**

237. Base of picture 236.

238. Pair continental
figures **£40** €**56**

239. Four Lladro figures
£40 €**56**

240. Pair china poodles
£50 €**70**

241. Beswick figure "Thrush"
£40 €**56**

Cheaper than Chips

243. Moorcroft vase **£150** €210

244. Three Wade miniatures **£40** €56

246. Poole pottery vase **£50** €70

245. Base of picture 246.

247. Collection of Wade **£45** €63

248. Clarice Cliff vase & plate **£100** €140

249. Royal Dux figure of a ballerina **£40** €56

250. Continental painted plate **£60** €84

251. Moorcroft vase **£180** €252

Clarice Cliff

(1899 - 1972) ...

...started her craft of free hand painting at an early age in 1916. At the age of 17 she joined Wilkinsons where she spent her entire career. The brightly coloured designs became known as bizarre ware, her colourful leafy designs and homely scenes became very popular through the art deco period and were mass-produced. Rare pieces can fetch thousands of pounds today, but be aware that many pieces now produced are copies.

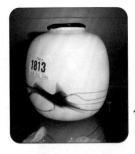

1325. Black/white studio glass jar **£40 €56**

326. Victorian "God Speed The Plough" mug **£45 €63**

1327. Musical 'John Peel' jug **£30 €42**

1328. Doulton Lambeth posy vase & 2 red glass dishes **£30 €42 and £100 €140**

1329. Staffordshire Spill vase figure **£60 €84**

1330. Staffordshire Montgomery jug **£20 €28**

1331. Toby jug **£10 €14**

1332. Royal Copenhagen mug **£35 €49**

HY07. Preserves jar with wax cap **£5 €7**

HY08. Q.E.2 miniature whisky jug **£5 €7**

1335. 3 Treen items **£20 €28**

1336. Clarice Cliff clog & Beswick figure of 2 terriers **£50 €70 and £60 €84**

Cheaper than Chips

1337. Small Royal Doulton character jug 'Bootmaker' & Royal Doulton 'Rose' **£22 €30 and £35 €49**

1338. Beswick Double Diamond advertising figure **£45 €63**

1339. Myott vase **£75 €105**

1340. Early 20c. 3 piece Japanese cruet **£15 €21**

1341. Pair Hydra jugs **£80 €112**

1342. 'Smugglers' plaque **£40 €56**

1346. Moorcroft box cover **£105 €146**

HY09. 3 Cauldon egg cups **£20 €28**

HY10. Fine porcelain & gilt cup **£5 €7**

Prattware

The first examples of Prattware date back to 1775 but the warm colours of the lead-glazed Cream ware of Staffordshire were soon copied by many. Water jugs, tableware, plaques and many commemorative items and figures were produced using blue green and browns. Highly decorative items fetch good money and are popular with dealers and collectors.

HY12. Q.E.2 Silver jubilee glass mug **£5 €7**

1348. Copeland butter dish **£30 €42**

1349. Royal Doulton figure 'Laura' **£75 €105**

1350. Midwinter egg cruet **£20 €28**

1351. Royal Doulton Bunnykins warming dish **£55 €77**

1352. Green Carnival glass bowl on stand **£30 €42**

HY13. Brass box tea caddie **£10 €14**

LM35. Sadler staffs. 'Hamlet' teapot **£15 €21**

1355. Pratt ware type Claret jug **£50 €70**

1356. Beswick cat **£30 €42**

1357. Base of Beswick cat

1358. 3 Flying ducks **£15 €21**

1359. 6 Bottle condiment **£40 €56**

Cheaper than Chips

252. Box Wade miniatures
£50 €**70**

253. Figures at a wishing well
£50 €**70**

255. Two Wedgewood lilac
Jasperware items **£30** €**42**

254. Wade pipe rest
£30 €**42**

256. Royal Doulton Art Nouveau
jug and bowl **£80** €**112**

257. Two Meat dishes
£40 €**56**

258. Flow blue toilet jug &
bowl **£90** €**126**

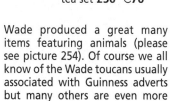

259. Wedgewood
tea set **£50** €**70**

LM12. 'Christmas tree'
by Hadida
£10 €**14**

Top Tips

Wade produced a great many items featuring animals (please see picture 254). Of course we all know of the Wade toucans usually associated with Guinness adverts but many others are even more valuable. To name a couple Si and Am, two Wade Disney cats at over £400 the pair. Wade made quite a few products for public houses over the years such as ashtrays, water jugs and even bottles for Whisky etc.

1363. Victorian plated teapot **£30** €**42**

1360. Cut glass Epergne **£30** €**42**

1361. Oval tray 3 piece service **£15** €**21**

1362. Horn handled fish servers **£20** €**28**

1364. Plated coffee pot **£20** €**28**

1365. Early 19c. cut glass hip flask **£35** €**49**

1366. Sheffield plate Baluster water jug **£40** €**56**

1367. Plated cocktail flask **£40** €**56**

1368. 3 Silver backed brushes and hand mirror **£40** €**56**

1369. Boxed tea/coffee set, silver plate. **£80** €**112**

HY01. T.G. Green & Co. the Gripstand mixing bowl **£30** €**42**

1371. Wilesco steam factory **£70** €**98**

Cheaper than Chips

1372. 2 boxes fish servers
£50 €70

1373. Paragon tea service
with silver beakers in box
£150 €210

1374. Art Deco period
canteen of cutlery
£80 €112

1375. Victorian fish servers
£45 €63

1376. Tea kettle on stand
with burner
£45 €63

1377. Bristol blue bottle
with sherry label
£30 €42

1378. Cast brass single
bottle inkstand
£40 €56

1379. Inlaid banded needlework
box £70 €98

1380. Inside pic 1379.

Cheaper than Chips

Glass and iron brought together was a popular design feature from the early Victorian era right through to the art deco period of the 1920's and 1930's. This was mainly due to the versatility of both products and the industrial revolution, both being easy and cheap to produce. However, some good examples are worth collecting. See picture 266.

261. Walnut wall clock **£160** €**224**

262. Walnut Dropdial wall clock **£260** €**365**

263. Pair hand bellows **£35** €**49**

264. Browning box camera **£45** €**63**

265. Pair oriental bronzed vases on stand **£110** €**154**

266. Glass & wrought iron light shade **£50** €**70**

267. Sylvac posy pot, Tree stump & Fawn **£40** €**56**

268. Telephone **£50** €**70**

269. Banjo in case **£60** €**84**

270. Woodworking plane **£30** €**42**

Cheaper than Chips

1381. Mahogany Tambour top stationery box **£70** €98

1382. Inside pic 1381.

1383. Brass framed 4 glass mantel clock with mercury pendulum **£140** €196

1384. Oak Tambour top stationery box **£50** €70

1385. Inside pic 1384.

1386. Dog and bowl vesta stand, pewter teapot and pepper pot **£25** €35 **and £20** €28

1387. Hand held storm lantern **£20** €28

1388. Mahogany microscope slide cabinet and slides **£200** €280

1389. Brass 2 bottle inkstand **£25** €35

Tambour Tops...

...are made up of many pieces of wood interlocked together to give a curved finish to the overall appearance of the piece. Very popular with writing desks the normally hard wood Tambour was made from woods such as oak or mahogany. And because of the durability of these woods there is still a steady supply of these writing or stationary boxes around. Well made and looked after examples will bring a good return on your investment.

1390. 19c. 2 bottle
ink well
£30 €42

1391. Pntd W/C scrolling
picture temple
subjects **£50 €70**

1392. Oak brush
box **£40**
€56

1393. Inside pic 1392.

1394. Coal
perdonium
£45 €63

1395. Brass barrel
scuttle
£65 €91

1396. Pair Adlake
engine lamps
£100 €140

1397. Small jewel box
£30 €42

1398. Brass
carriage clock
£70 €98

1399. 1950's dressing table tray,
2 candlestick porcelain vases
£25 €35

1400. Mantel clock
£50 €70

1401. Slate and marble
mantel clock with
figure Mount
£130 €182

Cheaper than Chips

1402. Rhenish type 2 hand vase
£45 €63

1403. Copper kettle with white porcelain handle
£45 €63

1404. 4 Mahogany head wig and gown carriers
£35 €49

1405. Brass kettle and ladle
£25 €35

1406. Brass firestand & tools
£40 €56

1407. Elephant foot jardinière
£80 €112

1408. 3 Biscuit tins
£35 €49

1409. Embossed copper scuttle **£55 €77**

1410. Arthur Wood vase and Lladro figure 'Japanese geisha girl'
£30 €42 and £35 €49

1411. Doulton Lambeth bowl
£35 €49

Cheaper than Chips

Top Tips

Collectors of kitchenalia are enjoying something of a boom and the variety of items coming onto the market never seems to stop. From old cast irons to kitchen scales, bread bins and utensils. Although these items do not have much use other than decoration, they can add that desired look in a country style kitchen or a public house. Although nostalgic, as we move into the 21st century they do not offer much more than this.

271.4 Buick hub caps
£50 €70

272. Part liqueur set **£20 €28**

273. Pan scale
£45 €63

274. Poole pottery vase
£45 €63

275.2 flat irons
£25 e35

276. Oriental figure
£25 €35

277. Devon teapot
£30 €42

278. Old radio
£40 €56

279. Pairs of carved metal 'Fighting cock' figures
£40 €56

Cheaper than Chips

1412. Poole Pottery vase **£140 €196**

1413. Base of pic 1412.

1414. Lemonade set **£30 €42**

1415. Clarice Cliff plate and vase **£40 €56**

1416. Base of pic 1415.

1417. 6 Bunnykins items **£30 €42**

HY14. Hawkeye-major six-20 box camera **£15 €21**

1419. Coloured glass clown **£15 €21**

1420. Staffordshire dog **£45 €63**

1421. 2 storage jars **£30 €42**

HY15. Kodak portrait brownie senior six-20 **£20 €28**

Cameras

The fascination that seems to go with cameras is with us all, whether looking back at old grainy photos of a bygone era, or the camera itself, it seems we all have an old camera hidden away in the loft or attic. The old box cameras that survive today though should give a small return, that's if you can bear to part with it. There are some collectors around who will buy working models. Better to look out for more modern examples from the 50's & 60's.

1423. 2 decanters
& stoppers
£30 €42

1424. Beswick serving dish
£25 €35

1425. Base of
pic 1424.

1426. Pair Sherry
decanters & stoppers
£35 €49

1427. R/Dux
figure of girl
£45 €63

1428. R/Dux figure
of nude girl
£70 €98

1429. Blue/white
Spode jar & cover
£50 €70

1430. Royal Doulton character
jug 'The Huntsman'
£45 €63

1431. R/Dux figure
of ballerina
£65 €91

HY16. Continental
figure group
£15 €21

1434. Coalport figure
£30 €42

1435. Base of
pic 1434.

Cheaper than Chips

1432. Bunnykins 2 handled mug, cup, saucer, bowls 2 plates & Wedgewood plate **£35 €49**

1436. Ship's clock **£65 €91**

1437. Anniversary clock under glass dome **£65 €91**

1438. Gilt metal 2 handled urn **£22 €31**

1440. Seiko mantel clock **£80 €112**

1439. Metamec mantel clock **£25 €39**

1442. Pair continental porcelain figures **£100 €140**

1443. Bierstein tankard **£20 €28**

1444. Costa glass vase **£50 €70**

1445. C S Adams preserve pot, Poole Pottery items **£30 €42**

1441. 8 Collectors' plates
£75 €105

1446. 4 Bowls,
7 stands
£20 €28

1447. 4 Green Majolica dishes
£40 €56

1448. Copeland
'Churchill' character
jug **£40 €56'**

HY17. Robert Sydenham
vase
£10 €14

1450. Poole Pottery
vase **£30 €42**

1451. Base of
pic 1450.

1452. Pair Devon vases
£20 €28

1453. Royal Doulton series
ware part tea set
£50 €70

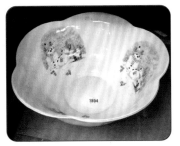

1455. Royal Worcester
bowl Snowman
£40 €56

1456. Base of pic 1455
Royal Worcester.

Cheaper than Chips

280. Old telephone
£30 €**42**

281. Old telephone
£30 €**42**

282. Sewing machine
£30 €**42**

283. Baluster vase
£35 €**49**

284. Moorland cottage jug
£40 €**56**

285. Pair binocular **£30**
€**42**

286. Gramophone
£75 €**105**

287. 5 model cars
£60 €**84**

288. Coalport "Lady Tennis
Player" **£50** €**70**

289. Base of figure pic 288.

The almost certain demise of the household telephone has brought thousands of these items to auction and car-boot sales. Although I think some of the early Bakelite ones will have quaintness about them, big companies have been throwing them away for decades. A good tip is to find a couple of good coloured Bakelite examples not the black ones and store them as possible bargains of the future (perhaps the distant future). However, it is not advised to do this with the early mobile telephones, as the batteries may become unstable.

1454. Spode 'Bridge' coffee set **£50 €70**

1457. Green overlaid glass basket & blue bowl **£80 €112**

1458. Hammersley 'Strawberries & Cream' set **£30 €42**

1459. Ducal part dinner service **£80 €112**

1460. Pair Oriental chargers **£40 €56**

1461. Blue/white meat platter **£80 €112**

1462. Base of pic 1461 Rileys China.

1463. Porcelain coffee set for 2 on tray **£50 €70**

1464. C/Ducal dinner service **£80 €11**

Cheaper than Chips

1465. Pair Venetian style wall mirrors **£600 €840**

1466. Pair Venetian style wall mirrors **£600 €840**

1467. Wall clock **£50 €70**

HY18. Smoker's pipe horn & Bakelite A/S **£15 €21**

1468. 6 Spitting Image white glazed items **£60 €84**

1470. Lorna Bailey sugar sifter **£50 €70**

1471. Lorna Bailey cream jug **£38 €53**

1474. 2 Lorna Bailey pieces, milk jug and sugar **£38 €53**

1475. Poole Pottery vase **£38 €53**

1476. Base of pic 1475.

Moorland/Chelsea

The Moorland Chelsea works at Burslem really is a continuation of hundreds of years of fine pottery works coming out of Staffordshire. The pictures on page 129 show work associated with Susie Cooper, after the death of Josheph Szeiler who owned the site from 1957 to 1986.

The Moorland Pottery Company took over the site and started producing a fine line of highly coloured designs for tableware etc. Moorland pottery is very collectable; especially designs by Suzie Cooper like the 'Crocus' pattern.

HY19. H.Grindly & Co. satin white
ironstone teapot
£20 €28

1477. Chelsea mug
Moorland
£25 €35

1478. Base of
Chelsea
mug.

1479. Art Deco
style vase
£38 €53

1481. 3 piece tea set
£15 €21

1482. Base of
pic 1481.

1483. Moorland 'Crocus'
pattern jug
£40 €56

1484. Base of pic 1483
Moorland 'Crocus'.

HY20. Ovaltine pottery
Silver Jubilee mug
£7 €10

1485. Mandolin
in case
£35 €49

1486. Inside of
pic 1485.

1487. Special edition
Aston Martin
£10 €14

HY21. Shelly jug
£20 €28

Cheaper than Chips

290. Wade Christmas teapot **£25** €35

291. Base of picture 290.

292. 2 brass railway carriage lamps + oil lamp **£65** €90

293. Green onyx telephone **£40** €56

294. Enfield oak cased mantel clock **£45** €63

295. Brass desk stand **£30** €42

296. A pair of ship lamps **£80** €112

297. A pair china liqueur bottles **£20** €28

298. A set of enamelled kitchen scales **£20** €28

Top Tips

Ship's lamps are another nostalgic item from a bygone era but these will have a good return value to the collector. They are usually well made and have plenty of brass on them and once cleaned can be safely used in the home or garden. Be sure to use the correct paint etc. if using with candles, as they become rare.

299. Chandelier **£15** €**21**

Cheaper than Chips

Trunks and boxes, examples of the one pictured in 306 seem to be on the wane. They have few uses in our modern homes and are even clumsy for storage. Leave these to the theme pubs and save your money until you see a nice oak blanket box. It will cost you but will never devalue and you can use it every day.

300. Chandelier
£25 €**35**

301. Chandelier
£20 €**28**

302. Chandelier
£20 €**28**

303. Chandelier
£20 €**28**

304. Chandelier
£20 €**28**

305. Enamel bread bin,
circa 1960's **£35** €**49**

306. Dome topped trunk
£40 €**56**

307. Oak swing mirror
£40 €**56**

308. Table top stationary cabinet,
tambour front **£38** €**53**

Cheaper than Chips

1490. Beswick character jug
£25 €39

1491. Base of pic 1490 Beswick.

1492. 3 Storage jars
£20 €28

1493. Poole Pottery vase
£45 €63

1494. Flat iron with block
£25 €39

1495. Gramophone with brass horn
£50 €70

1496. Stone flour bin
£20 €28

1497. Old radio
£25 €39

1498. Saddle
£40 €56

1499. Mandolin in carry case
£30 €42

Leatherwork

Items of leatherwork like saddles and horse riding equipment do not come to auctions or the car-boot sale often. Probably because of the amount of wear that in its normal life it has endured. Good examples of worked leather can be turned into a small profit at sales, because the cost of purchasing good quality leather is prohibitive, so if you can find them I suggest a small mark up after a good leather treatment.

1500. Croquet set in box
£100 €140

1501. Wall clock
£50 €70

1502. Wall clock
£50 €70

1503. Accordion in case
£35 €49

1504. Bagatelle board
£75 €105

1505. Set chimes
£40 €56

1506. Bagatelle board
£50 €70

1507. Set of Salter scales brass face and bowl
£40 €56

1508. Warming pan
£30 €42

1509. Frys Cocoa old tin sign
£50 €70

1510. Wooden rocking horse
£20 €28

1511. Scales & weights
£20 €28

Cheaper than Chips

1512. 1930's enamel stove £70 €98

1513. Trouser press £20 €28

1514. Swinging clown £20 €28

1515. Oriental plated, pierced pot £15 €21

1516. Early 20c. French parasol £40 €56

1517. Soft toy Koala bear £25 €35

1519. Mountain goat & tree epergne stand £50 €70

1520. Pair candlesticks £40 €56

1518. Bottle coaster, basket, egg condiment stand £35 €49

1521. Brass 4lb weight £20 €28

1522. White stone and Malachite chess set £25 e35

Cheaper than Chips

Top Tips

Brass instruments seem to be in good supply including theodolites, compasses, sextants etc. The market for these will probably remain strong. They are usually well made and if you don't mind a bit of elbow grease now and then, they look good too. A nice telescope for £60 will still be worth £60 in five years, but just think of the star-gazing pleasure in that time!

309. A brass Gunsight with stand **£100** €140

310. A brass compass **£38** €53

311. A temple mantel clock **£80** €112

312. Two percussion revolvers **£150 £80,** €210 €112

313. An engraved glass Epergne in a carved wood stand **£60** €84

314. Pair of open twist brass candle stick **£30** €42

315. Black leather cased Clock **£40** €56

317. Carved wood box **£30** €42

Cheaper than Chips

1523. Carved African woman **£38 €53**

1524. 2 Rhino heads carved black wood **£24 €33**

1525. Flowery milk jug 'Bloomers' **£10 €14**

1526. Pair Aynsley cottage garden plates **£10 €14 each**

1527. Pair ornate brass picture frames **£48 €67**

1528. Pair brass candlesticks **£28 €39**

1529. Wooden carved chicken **£8 €11**

1530. Large turkey meat plate **£28 €39**

1531. Coopered ewer **£16 €22**

1532. Brooks & Bentley vase **£10 €14**

Claret Jugs/ Decanters

It's always worth casting an eye over these objects if you come across them at sales, as there are both collectors of glass and silver. And these classic items can fulfil the needs of both and good examples of crystal and silver jugs or decanters will usually prove to be a good investment. However, avoid pressed or moulded glass and silver-plated objects or it will be you who is supplying the profit to another party.

1533. Pair wooden candlesticks **£12 €17**

1534. Claret jug **£12 €17**

1535. Blue and white hand painted vase **£18 €25**

1536. Smoked glass jug **£12 €17**

1537. Gold coloured Art Deco lady **£18 €25**

1538. Royal Albert cup and saucer **£4 €6**

1539. Brass eagle on marble base **£10 €14**

1540. Brass horn **£12 €17**

1541. Yellow bird jug **£16 €22**

1542. 2 Small cast iron urns **£10 €14 each**

1543. Pair china elephants **£24 €33**

1544. Hand painted vase **£12 €17**

Cheaper than Chips

1545. 2 Compartment fairy pot 'Braithwaites' **£32 €44**

1546. Coffee grinder – softwood brass inlay **£8 €11**

1547. Blue Victorian Procelain figure **£12 €17**

1548. Crystal cut glass fruit bowl **£22 €30**

1551. Brass candlestick **£18 €25**

1549. ,Paussey pot & coffee cups, 'View near Greenwich' **£10 €14 each**

1550. Ginger and Temple jars **£5-8 €7-11 each**

1552. Mason's meat plate **£32 €44**

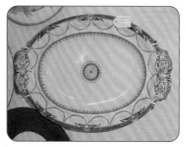

1553. Copeland dish **£5 €7**

1554. Crown Devon plate **£6 €8**

CHELSEA PORCELAIN 1744-1784

Nicholas Sprimont, a French silversmith came to England to seek his fortune. He was a registered silversmith in London from 1741.

From 1743 to 1747 he produced 15 pieces most of which are now in fine art museums. When Chelsea was just a village in Middlesex, he established the Chelsea factory making wares and ornamental pieces from porcelain. Many of these wares were copies of, or heavily influenced by the designs coming out of Meissen Porcelain (Dresden). He even borrowed pieces from the English Ambassador at Dresden to copy.

Other first pieces of porcelain manufactured were direct copies of the silverwork he had previously designed, for instance a silver crayfish on a rocky base.

THE TRIANGLE PERIOD 1743-1749

Typical of this period were shallow oval like dishes, some applied with berries or leaves often called strawberry dishes. Some of these have added leaves or insects painted on them to hide blemishes or firing faults. Other pieces of this time include shell forms of salt and peppershakers, or extremely rare a centerpiece of 3 shells around a knot of coral stems. Also a few rare examples of human, bird and animal figures.

The factory closed for a year in 1749, it is believed during this time it was expanded and reorganized.

THE RAISED ANCHOR PERIOD 1750-1752

This period sees more use of enamelling, and covers the 'Girl in a swing' period (most wares of which are held in museums). Items produced were mainly small ornamental snuff boxes and figures (63 different ones produced in this period) recognized by their naive quality, rustic charm and simplicity. The porcelain paste and similarities of the form of modelling mainly identify this period. Things to look out for are the characters distinctive heads, straight Grecian style of noses, deep set eyes and small hands and feet. The Porcelain has a dense cool appearance and the clear glaze a tinge of green. Pieces are set on a natural looking base or bevelled in and out.

In this period the first of the 'Chelsea moons' appear, lighter spots of transparency, shown by transmitted light in the greenish yellow tone of the body. These are air bubbles trapped in the paste at the mixing stage. This feature stops in 1758 when boneash becomes a new ingredient. Some wares produced were totally plain; others have Japanese painted figures or images. There are also conventional floral designs and 'Fable painting'.

RED ANCHOR WARES 1752-1758

This period sees the finest body of wares produced.

Occasionally these will have the 'moons'. The surface colours ranged from cool white to greyish cream, sometimes with a bluish tinge in the glaze.

In 1756 the glaze becomes more transparent, sometimes with a crazed surface. Popular shapes included the 'Hollowware', a range of leaf molded bowls (i.e. cabbage, fig, lettuce and vine), finger bowls and water cups. Small tureens also feature, in various animal shapes, coloured according to nature, and some of these can be the most desirable to a collector. The largest are in the form of full-grown animals and fish, often sold in pairs and looking as lifelike as they could. Examples are hen and chickens; double pigeon and plaice with fish tailed handles.

Sir Hans Sloane was noted to have decorated porcelain with a botanical theme. The 'Fable 'series continued, notably the later piece feature clouds in the sky.

RED ANCHOR FIGURES

139 different figures were produced in this period, and are thought to be the finest of the factory creations, and command a price to match. Types include; Cries of Paris, beggars, pastoral/peasant groups, seasons, senses and elements. to name a few.

GOLD ANCHOR 1759-1769

This period continued with a more elaborate and colorfully decorated selection, with increased use of guilding. The finish tended to be fine and white with a thick glassy tinge, however the glaze often crazed badly, gathering in hollows with a greenish yellow or blue tinge. This soft glaze easily scratched or rubbed.

The figures carried on in much the same themes as before, with the most celebrated being the Ranelagh Masqueraders.

Tureens were plainer than before and there was an introduction of large handled beakers decorated with painted birds and flowers; figures would be laid in chiselled gold. Many of these were made for display rather than use.

Vases were issued in pairs or sets (known as garnitures) of 3, 5 or 7 with the central piece the largest, then pairs descending in size. Chelsea-Derby years 1770-1784.

In 1769 Sprimont sold the factory to James Cox, who passed it on the Duesbury and Heath (Manufacturers of Porcelain in Derby). Duesbury had no tradition of the manufacture of porcelain. The pieces were now decorated by both Chelsea and Derby, continuing with Sprimont's designs. However the Derby influence gradually took over the Chelsea style over the next 15 years, until it finally ceased production all together with the sale of the factory in 1783.

MARKS

Triangle period: marks are rare, however you do find the occasional crown and trident mark with a blue underglaze.

Raised Anchor, these marks tend to be with a rounded crown and double barbed flukes. Numerals are added to facilitate matching between lid and base of tureens. Usually placed just inside the Fortnum on wares and on the back and upper part of figure base. Colour variations are some blue on wares, or a blue underglaze with overglaze of red and green and guilding. Gold Anchor, has angular crown and down pointing barbs. On some small figures a double anchor mark appears.

Chelsea-Derby period, now a D appears with the anchor straight through the vertical, usually in gold. From 1773-82 the crown appears above the D, sometimes with an N.

COLLECTING

Knowledge of the types of pastes used is really essential and this can only be done by handling the pieces, not in museums! This is not a cheap range to collect!

It is possible however to collect pieces from each Chelsea period even with marks. Small amounts of damage will obviously affect the price, but not necessarily spoil a display. Wares are less expensive, and more easily available. Figures of the red anchor period are very rare and priced accordingly!

To obtain a piece of Chelsea is to have the thrill of owning something which comes from the earliest days of porcelain manufacture -made by one of the most prestigious factories of the 18th century.

COPIES

Best known are those of the Gold anchor figures and candlesticks made by Messrs, Samson of Paris. Samson productions are also collected in their own right. Molds were taken from originals, so they tend to be slightly smaller, frequently with no mark, although sometimes a gold anchor will appear.

Another factory to 'copy' was Sitzendorf in Thuringia (German Factories).

0107R&D Two pairs of hand decorated vases
£80 €112 each pair

0110R&D Heavy copper/ brass fireside bin
£125 €175

0113R&D Carlton ware leaf shaped fruit bowl
£55 €77

0120R&D Transfer printed Dutch scene blue & white planter
£35 €49

0127R&D Two Brass shell casings 250mm
£70 €98

1555. Jackson Goslin
plate, 1914. **£10 €14**

1556. Copeland Spode
plate **£25 €35**

1557. Copeland plate
£8 €11

1558. Sylvac jug,
stork handle
£45 €63

1559. Booths plate
£6 €8

1560. Silver plated
coffee pot
£22 €30

1561. Blue and white tile
£8 €11

1562. Pair Faience
candlesticks
£55 €77

1563. Coalport plate
£8 €11

1564. Coalport plate
£4 €6

1565. Old Chelsea
Crown pottery
£18 €25

Cheaper than Chips

1566. Faience match holder and pot **£10 €14 each**

1567. Rouen dish **£10 €14**

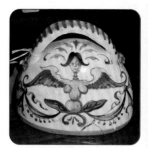

1568. Faience bell **£8 €11**

1569. Devon ware teapot **£40 €56**

1570. Devon ware coffee pot **£22 €30**

1572. Hornsey with squirrels **£14 €20**

1571. Honiton pottery **£14 €20**

1573. Rouen blue and white candle holder **£15 €21**

1574. Copeland Spode dish **£12 €17**

1575. Spode jug **£38 €53**

Cheaper than Chips

1576. Blue and white scene plate **£6** €8

EARLY EARTHENWARE...

...was produced in cobalt and even black and reds. Purples or brown are normally attributed to the Victorian era, particularly Mason ironstone and Spode from 1813.

Ironstone was extremely hard and cheap to produce; although probably not the most decorative example it was very durable and even early examples survive in good condition.

1577. Wedgewood plate **£6** €8

1578. Set small tea knives **£10** €14

1579. Anchor pottery cheese dish **£22** €30

1580. Sutherland cup and saucer **£15** €21

1581. Allcock sauce dish and ladle **£22** €30

1582. Indian tree tea pot **£12** €17

1583. Silver plated tray **£18** €25

1584. 2 Mason's pudding dishes 'Regency' **£6** €8 **for pair**

1585. 2 Mason's saucers 'Regency' **£4** €6 **each**

Cheaper than Chips

1596. Black Forest clock circa 1910 **£25 €35**

1586. KLM Delft tankard **£8 €11**

1587. Holkham studio pottery Norfolk **£16 €22**

1589. Limoges tureen **£38 e53**

1590. Commemorative Jean Paul II chalice **£8 €11**

1591. Palissy plate (Royal Worcester Spode) **£8 €11**

1592. Ceramic barrel **£26 e36**

1593. Hand painted Portugese bowl **£12 €17**

1588. Avery kitchen scale and weights **£20 €28**

1595. 8 Day German wall clock **£65 €91**

1597. Tunstall vase **£5 €7**

1598. Ironstone plate **£12 €17**

Limoges Pottery & Porcelain

Limoges pottery takes its name from the area of France where the clay is quarried. From 1736 this clay was used at the Sevres factory. Other hard paste porcelain factories have been setting up in the area ever since. Limoges sent most of its pottery to the Sevres for decoration. Faience pottery was also made at Limoges from as early as 1736. Look out for Cd incised or painted marks or Limoges added in red.

1594. Old carved box
£8 €**11**

1599. Spode plate
£10 €**14**

1600. Embroidered
fire screen
£15 €**21**

1601. Sandland cricket
mug circa 1950
£12 €**17**

1604. Royal Doulton
jug **£25** €**35**

1602. Faience dish
£10 €**14**

1603. Sadler egg cups
£2 €**3**

1605. Lord Nelson jug
£15 €**21**

1606. Baxters
marmalade pot
£6 €**8**

1607. Copper inkwell
£10 €**14**

1608. Mason's Ironstone
milk jug **£15** €**21**

Cheaper than Chips

318. Two pewter tankards
£40 €56

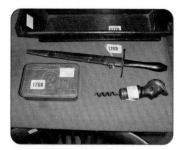

319. First world war chocolate tin, a cruciform
dagger and a jockey corkscrew
£20 £45 £20 €28 €63 €28

320. A Georgian cutlery
tray **£60 €84**

321. Bevelled glass panelled
lantern **£80 €112**

322. Two copper bed warming pans
£40 each, €56 each

323. A brass kettle on stand
with burner **£45 €63**

316. A horn with metal mounts and
a Chieftain's Whisk candle
£40 £40 €56 €56

325. A selection of lead
soldiers **£40 €56**

326. A selection of lead
soldiers **£40 €56**

Lead
Soldiers...

...can be found in most households. They are collectable and people buy them, repaint them and restore them to their true condition. A good solid collectable for anyone looking for worthwhile items, some are valuable.

324. A small oak mantel clock **£40** **€56**

1609. Box fish knives and forks **£16** **€22**

1610. Milner tin box **£12** **€17**

1611. Cut glass vinegar bottle **£12** **€17**

1612. Glass bird ornaments **£10** **€14** **each**

1613. Mason's cup and saucer 'Regency' **£10** **€14**

1614. Mason's tea pot 'Regency' **£15** **€21**

1615. Round mosaic box **£10** **€14**

1616. Oak letter rack **£7** **€10**

1617. Brass desk top lamp **£22** **€30**

1618. Pen holder & note pad **£10** **€14**

1619. Bust of Apollo (not marble) **£10** **€14**

Cheaper than Chips

1620. Cut glass scent bottle **£9 €13**

1621. Old Folly shoe **£7 €10**

1622. Jane Asher limited edition box **£12 €17**

1623. Glue pot **£8 €11**

1625. Allerton jug **£18 €25**

1624. Old car horn, brass **£24 €33**

1628. Italian design wall plate **£22 €30**

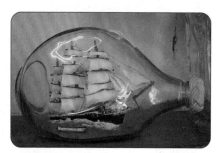

1626. Cutty Sark in bottle **£18 €25**

1627. Large glass bowl **£25 €35**

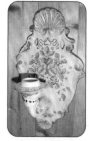

1629. Derouta wall candle holder **£10 €14**

Car Memorabilia

Car memorabilia has and always will be collectable. Old lamps, horn's, badges and the like attract quite a following all over the world. These can easily be sold on the Internet, so it's worth a punt if you come across any nice pieces. Car badges can be particularly valuable - old MG or BENTLY for example, but lesser known or old names are just as sought after.

1630. Victorian tureen
£20 €28

1631. Early 20c. Wedgewood salad bowl **£42 €56**

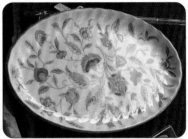

1632. Minton Hadham Hall bone china
£8 €11

1633. Ridgeway bowl Mid 20c.
£10 €14

1634. Old copper warming pan
£68 €95

1635. Brass shell case circa 1916
£22 €30

1636. Umbrella stand wood and brass
£22 €30

1637. Old cased bridge set
£6 €8

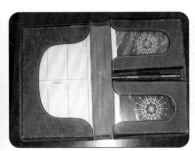

1637. Old cased bridge set
£6 €8

1639. Pair ebony candlesticks
£6 €8

1640. Brass and copper vase **£12 €17**

Cheaper than Chips

327. A selection of lead soldiers **£40 €56**

328. A selection of lead soldiers **£40 €56**

329. A selection of lead soldiers **£40 €56**

330. An oak biscuit barrel **£40 €56**

331. A silver photo frame and a pierced basket **£45 £55 €63 €77**

332. A silver photo frame **£80 €112**

333. Two entree dishes and covers **£80 €112**

334. Four candle sticks, silver on copper **£80 €112**

335. A four piece tea and coffee service & tray **£80 €112**

Cheaper than Chips

Royal Dalton's figures are hugely popular and these valuations may anger many collectors. They are good pieces but there is some uncertainty about the strength of the market, which appears solid even though so many pieces are traded. They are available at auctions and carboot sales and can fetch £100.

337. A chamber stick
£30 €42

336. A magnifying glass **£10 €14**

339. Oriental taper stand box and cover **£40 €56**

338. A Victorian Salva candle snuffer Candelabrum **£50 €70**

340. Six fish knives and forks in a black leather box
£30 €42

341. Royal Doulton figures of Loretta & Winsome
£45 each €63 each

LM16. Royal Doulton 'Christmas day' 2002, HN4422
£100 €140

LM17. Royal Doulton 'Christmas day' 2001 HN4315
£100 €140

345. China tea pot
£20 €28

LM18. Royal Doulton 'Specially for you' HN4232
£100 €140

Cheaper than Chips

1641. Royal Venton
jam pot
£8 €11

1642. Wooden barometer
£12 €17

1643. Set of 3
horse brasses
£3 €4

1644. Stanley pottery
'Lilly' mug
£8 €11

1645. 1930's moulded
glass ceiling light
£22 €30

1646. Stoneware vase
£45 €63

1648. 19c. European
cranberry dish
£60 €84

1647. Royal Worcester
mug **£28 €39**

1649. Portmerion oval dish
£14 €20

1650. Gillhiston
pottery vase
£12 €17

1651. Pair foreign china
hunting boot flasks
£18 €25

Lighting

Old-fashioned lighting also appears to do quite well at car boot sales and auction rooms. Although not terribly expensive their period designs are sought after. The materials that they have been constructed from can usually be of a high quality, and with many pieces from the 1940's, 50's and 60's the Art Deco theme also helps them along.

1652. AGFA Karat Comper camera **£26** €**36**

1653. Dartmouth jug **£12** €**17**

1654. Scales **£10** €**14**

1655. Royal Crown Derby 'Mikado' plate **£16** €**22**

1656. Cold cast bronze **£14** €**20**

1657. Bread bin **£15** €**21**

1658. Brass milk urn **£55** €**77**

1659. Chinese tea service **£35** €**49**

1660. Copper urn **£110** €**154**

1661. Chest tea caddy **£33** €**46**

1662. Silver plated tea caddy **£35** €**49**

1664. Cast of warrior **£120** €**168**

Cheaper than Chips

1663. Inkwell circa 1890
£48 €67

1665. Kirkhams
decanter & cups
£22 €30

1666. Figure
of jester
£28 €39

1667. Cut glass decanter
and stopper
£25 €35

1668. Napolean
tea pot
£18 €25

1669. Clock money box
'Time to save'
£15 €21

1670. The Symplexophon,
circa 1910.
£45 €63

1671. Jelly mould (pottery)
£18 €25

1672. Old lantern
£36 €51

1673. Brass eagle
on mount
£12 €17

1674. Dartmouth dish
£10 €14

Carlton Ware produced by Wiltshaw and Robinson at the Carlton works, Stoke-On-Trent is featured in picture 355. This is a good example of Carlton Ware; they made various household products, for the kitchen especially. From 1925 onwards familiar items are of embossed salad or fruit bowls and marmalade, jam and salt and pepper pots. Pieces have a soft pastel appearance and can normally be found at car-boot sales for a few pounds. Carlton Ware did quite a bit of commission work also, again for the large breweries, many of these pieces can be worth £100's.

355. A Carlton ware dish
£20 €28

346. Two Beswick china
dogs **£30 €42**

347. Royal Doulton figures,
'Ballerina & Penny'
£45 each. € each

LM19. Royal Worcester Mistral
'Forces of creation'
£90 €126

349. Royal Albert china figures,
Beatrix potter **£50 €70**

350. Royal Doulton miniature jugs & figure
of a Spaniel **£35 each €49 each**

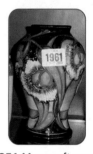

351. Moorcroft vase
£140 €196

352. A Royal Doulton
vase **£80 €112**

353. A Royal Doulton match pot & figure
Southern Belle **£20 £28 €90 €126**

354. A Moorcroft pot &
cover **£150 €210**

Cheaper than Chips

356. A miniature Royal Doulton figure of Monika **£35 €49**

LM11. 'The Leonardo collection Church' teapot, **£10 €14**

LM14. Porcelain 'Girl on tortoise' **£7 €10**

359. An oval Moorcroft box **£100 €140**

360. A Royal Copenhagen seated dog **£150 €210**

361. An onyx dish with Otter **£20 €28**

362. A Moorcroft vase with Puffins **£150 €210**

363. A pair of pen holders **£35 €49**

364. Two souvenir Isle of Man mugs **£25 €35**

Cheaper than Chips

1675. Hot water bottle – stoneware
£10 €14

1676. Stoneware hot water bottle
£10 €14

1677. Victorian gothic clock and alarm, circa 1880
£78 €109

1678. Austrian urn
£35 €49

1683. Cast iron and glass decanter **£16 €22**

1679. Muffin dish
£24 €33

1680. 'Shorter' butter dish **£18 €25**

1681. 'Shorter' jam pot
£18 €25

1682. Bicycle lamp
£18 €25

1684. Selection blue glass
£4 - £10 €6 - €14

1685. Carved Buddha
£11 €15

Cheaper than Chips

1686. Rabone tape measure
£18 €25

1687. Weaver's shuttle
£16 €22

1688. Bronze bust
£22 €30

1689. Oak framed
dinner gong
£36 €50

1690. Burlington ware
'Snuffy' toby jug
£28 €39

1691. Large number
stamp **£5 €7**

1692. Tiffany lamp
£78 €109

1693. Queen Victoria
bust **£60 €84**

1694. 1950 Crown Devon tea, sugar
and coffee jars **£38 €53**

1695. Pair Edwardian
Court ware plum vases
£38 €53

Commemorative Ware

Commemorative ware, as the name suggests, is collectable. Whether royal, or for state occasions many thousands of items have been produced. But a word of warning here: not to many of them are terribly valuable as thousands upon thousand of different designs could be produced for a Coronation or historic event. Therefore unless you particularly like one or two items as heirlooms, stick to well made pieces by renowned factories.

1696. Edward 8th
Coronation mug
Minton **£28** €**39**

1697. George 6th & Elizabeth
coronation mug
£12 €**17**

1698. Queen's Silver Jubilee
mug **£5** €**7**

1699. Queen's
Silver Jubilee
mug **£5** €**7**

1700. Carlton ware
dish **£28** €**39**

1701. Pair brass
candlesticks
£55 €**77**

1702. 19c. Bohemia
ruby vase
£48 €**67**

1704. Limoges
bon bon stand
£38 €**53**

1703. Old Libra scales and 7 weights
£48 €**67**

1705. Mirano vase
£48 €**67**

1706. Large brass
wall/fire place plaque
£20 €**28**

Cheaper than Chips

1707. Pair Pratt ware vases 1915
£50 €70

1709. Lustre bowl
£18 €25

1710. Poole salt & pepper pots
£9 €13

1708. Art Nouveau style vase
£38 €53

1711. Beswick dish
£10 €14

1712. Slipper pan
£12 €17

1715. Denby hot water jug (part of service)
£12 €17

1713. Carlton ware pot and stand **£10** €14

1714. Denby tea service
£30 €42

1716. Arthur Wood vase
£12 €17

1717. Royal Doulton posy
£20 €28

Coal Port...

...is also known as Coalbrookdale. This factory has been producing highly decorated vases, plates and dishes since around 1800. Typical pieces are hand painted over transfer items; of flower patterns and gilding. Very popular with those who like objects that catch the eye, Coal Port also produced a large number of commemorative items (please see picture 372) although this is quite a toned down example of Coal Port China. Marks to look for are CD, CDALE, CBD or Coalport or Coalbrookdale.

365. A plaster jar and cover £10 €14

366. A Woolpack tea pot £20 €28

367. Aidens Arms tea pot £20 €28

368. A carved wall mirror £60 €84

369. An oak framed wall mirror £45 €63

370. Circular carved mirror £50 €70

371. A gilt convex wall mirror £40 €56

372. A Coalport Silver Jubilee plate £30 €42

373. A Myott part dinner service £80 €112

Cheaper than Chips

1718. Heathcote Hall bone china posy
£12 €17

1719. Silk pictures
£4 €6 each

1720. Capstan dog
£16 €22

1721. Large Victorian coffee roaster
£33 €46

1722. 6 Crystal glasses
£22 €37

1723. Wade Bells Whisky bottle
£18 €25

1724. Soap stone vase
£8 €11

1725. Moulinette
£6 €8

1726. Bucket and drainer stoneware **£25 €35**

1727. Pair Oriental temple jars
£35 €49 for pair

1728. Bed warmer
£32 €44

1729. Victorian copper spirit kettle
£35 €49

1730. Pallisey coffee pot, bowl and jug
£8 €11

1731. Old Oxo tin **£4 €6**

1732. Old Edgeworth pipe tobacco tin
£5 €7

1733. Old meat grinder
£4 €6

1734. 19c. carved wood miniature boat
£70 €98

1735. 20c. Turned boxwood indicator bottle
£50 €70

1736. Killarney Yew wood inlaid bookstand
£70 €98

HY24. Solid silver forks & spoons
£3 € each

Cheaper than Chips

1738. Late 19c. travelling chess set in walnut box **£70 €98**

1739. Inside picture 1738.

1740. Regency gentleman's burr walnut travel box **£400 €560**

1741. Inside Regency travel box picture 1740.

1742. 19c. Red Boullework stationary box **£900 €1260**

1743. Regency rosewood 2 compartment tea caddy **£200 €280**

1744. Victorian dome topped burr walnut tea caddy **£180 €252**

1745. Victorian figured dome topped walnut box **£150 €210**

1746. Regency rosewood writing box **£150 €210**

Boxes & Tea Urns

Who can resist taking a long lingering look over the many high quality carved and inlaid boxes and tea urns produced by our forefathers. If you are looking to buy high quality and workmanship that is rare in today's market then look no further than investing in one of these. The condition of many of these boxes can be immaterial as long as the entire original piece still exists, as renovated boxes can fetch hundreds of pounds at Auction.

1747. Late Victorian Burr walnut writing stand **£140** €**196**

1748. Regency rosewood 2 compartment tea caddy **£180** €**252**

1749. Edwardian oak cigar box **£120** €**168**

1750. Late Swiss music box **£400** €**560**

1751. Inside music box picture 1750.

1752. Mid 19c. French portico clock in walnut **£180** €**252**

1753. Late 19c. German mantel clock **£140** €**196**

1754. Victorian arts & crafts copper lidded jug **£150** €**210**

1755. White onyx bell push **£40** €**56**

1756. Pair of marble ashtrays **£120** €**168**

1757. Victorian brass letter holder **£50** €**70**

Cheaper than Chips

374. An Oriental Warrier table lamp
£150 €210

375. A 19c. porcelain vase **£80 €112**

376. Cranberry glass dish with white overlay **£50 €70**

377. A pair of vases **£50 €70**

378. A white overlay candle sticks **£25 €35**

379. A Chinese porceline bowl **£35 €49**

380. A china flower posey **£10 €14**

381. A Wedgewood Jasper ware pot **£20 €28**

LM13. Miniature teapot **£5 €7**

385. Two china candlesticks **£20 €28**

Overlaid Glass...

...a technique producing such items as those featured in pictures 376 and 378, where two or more coloured glasses are fused together and then the outer layers are carved into producing the above effect. Well worth collecting, as it is a little unusual. Look out for the overlaid Cranberry glass items.

Cheaper than Chips

1758. 19c. Gilt metal paperweight
£30 €42

1759. 19c. Oriental bronze 2 handled urn **£120 €168**

1760. 19c. Russian brass water dispenser **£250 €350**

1761. French bust bronze 'Lady of Van de Straften' **£700 €980**

1762. 19c. Brass spirit lamps **£300 €420**

1763. 19c. Bronze Tazza signed A Richard **£300 €420**

1764. Late Georgian copper kettle **£40 €56**

HY23. Booths 'Real old willow' pattern.9072 A/F **£15 €21**

1766. 19c. Chinese famille jeune dish **£60 €84**

1767. 19c. Copeland meat drainer **£150 €210**

Cheaper than Chips

1768. Staffordshire figure 'Old Gentleman'
£70 €98

1769. Staffordshire clock figure group
£50 €70

1770. Staffordshire figures 'Watch Holder' and 'Basket Lady'
£120 and £80 e168 and €112

1771. Staffordshire spill vases
£120 €168

1772. Staffordshire figure group
£60 €84

1773. Staffordshire figure group
£140 €196

1774. Staffordshire figure group
£100 €140

1775. Staffordshire clock figure group
£60 €84

1776. White glazed continental rectangular dish
£80 €112

Flat-back Figures...

...were made basically to produce cheap items in their millions to the booming cottage construction of the Victorian age, designed to sit on mantel pieces or windows or even hung flat against the wall. Many Staffordshire potteries produced these from around the 19th century. Although their cheap mass production did little to save them gaining any real respectability as decorative objects. The fragile figures did not fare well and although many originals can fetch very good money, there are also many fake items on the market.

1777. Continental capped
vases & scent bottles
£150 €210

1778. Part Staffordshire
dessert service
£500 €700

HY34. Dartmouth
Devon planter
£20 €28

HY35. White glass & cover
German beer stein
£10 €14

HY36. 2 Glass 1960's
jelly moulds
£20 €28

HY37. Pair porcelain
wall pockets
£15 €21

HY38. Ovaltine & Horlicks
glass mixers
£15 €21

HY39. Axe Vale pottery
Devon
£20 €28

HY40. Bogris Holland wall
pocket circa 1904
£10 €14

HY41. 1920's brooch
£5 €7

MERRYTHOUGHT BEARS 1930 - PRESENT

In 1919 the spinning mill WG Holmes & GH Laxton imported raw mohair which they then spun and sold to the weavers of mohair cloth. In the mid 1930's there was a decline in the demand for mohair and Holmes and Laxton started Merrythought LTD, in Coalbrookdale, Shropshire. The company was started specifically to produce various soft toys, dolls and playthings in velvet, plush, wool and fur etc. Obviously this was an excellent market for the mohair.

The company brought in designers and staff whom had previously been involved with the toy market; this included one of the company's first designers, a Florence Attwood.

In 1931 there were 4 bears in the first catalogue, there were two traditional bears which were jointed in the classic way, and became widely known as Magnet bears. There were 4 sizes made from 31.5cm, to 61 cm in height with the 3 largest having auto-growl. The majority of these bears were sold for the young as playthings.

These were available in gold, sunkiss, mohair, light gold, art silk (in several different shades) and medium novelty quality. The bears ranged from about 30 to 66cm high going up in 2 or 3cm jumps.

The bears were at this stage just a part of a wide range of soft toys, which covered every imaginable kind of animal and dolls too. Various new bears were introduced to the catalogue every year, and were deleted from the catalogue (and production) as demand decreased. In the 1940's the production of the bears virtually ceased due to WW2 when the factory was put over the manufacture of gas masks etc. In 1942 there were only 5 new designs and only one of these was a bear.

By 1947 the factory was back in full production and the next year saw the bears being marketed by major London stores.

In the 1950's the bear's design changed slightly in that they tended to be made from 2 main pieces instead of the usual 4.

The bears were now being recorded, as 'series' there was the 'M' series, 'H' Series and 'L'.

Jean Barber replaced Florence Attwood as designer, and continued in this role until the mid 1960's, after which there was a succession of designers. During this time there was an increase in production of novelty and well known characters, such as Sooty and Yogi Bear (1962) of which there was a 28cm bear and the 68.5cm show piece which is very rare today. In 1966 Winnie the Pooh was launched, today this is a rare find with his red shirt still on.

In 1972 Jaqueline Revitt was mainly responsible for designing toys and collectable items. In the 70's the other UK manufacturers of soft bears began to compete with the incoming cheaper models from the Middle East. However Merryweather went the other way, stepping up quality, increasing the amount of fully jointed mohair bears in their catalogue, describing them as "best quality mohair". They also offered some bears in good quality synthetic fabrics, so they had something for every one. They also began to 'dress' bears more.

LIMITED EDITIONS

In 1983 Merryweather received a request from Tide-Rider, a small import business in America, for a limited number of signed bears for the growing US. Collectors market. At this time the collectors were going for the old style fully jointed mohair bears.

Jaqueline Revitt created 'The Edwardian', in 35.5 and 45.5cm heights, in short pile bright gold fur - but not in limited editions. This was only the one with antique style longer pile mohair, of which just 1,000 were made, boxed and numbered in sewn in labels, signed by the chairman, all for the US. Market.

The company went on to produce many more limited editions for the US market, all of which sold out. Examples of these are the Elizabethan bear and the Edwardian Surprise brown bear.

In 1990 the British collectors (indeed the rest of the world) were finally recognized, before this date they could only buy the limited edition bears through US retailers.

The first limited edition bear available throughout the world was the Diamond Jubilee bear, made to mark the 60th anniversary of the company. This bear was boxed and limited to just 2,500. He measures 45.5cm and is a classic fully jointed Ted, made from exclusive leather finish mohair with sueded cotton pads. He was launched at Harrods.

In 1991 the first international collectors catalogue was produced, some of the designs were unlimited, but most designs had about 500 made. The Micro-cheekys proved to be one of the most popular ranges (based on designs of the Classic cheeky which was one of the longest running designs from 1957-1986). There were 6 different finishes at 15cm high, and they would reappear as 'variations' in subsequent catalogues to keep up with demand.

COLLECTING

In 1995 the Merrythought International Collectors Club started, making one bear exclusively for them each year. Also many unusual ranges ranging from one-offs for silent auctions to inexpensive teddies for smaller budgets.

LABELS

Many designs did not appear in catalogues, being either made for major department stores or additional designs created after printing. Bears made for 'stores' may carry the store's name i.e. Harrods, JLP or Selfridges, but most often would just carry the Merrythought label.

There are a number of different labels, often found on one of the footpads. Old labels were often used on 'newer' models of bear, so they cannot be used to identify the time the bear was made.

In the 1930's celluloid covered metal button with Merrythoughts wishbone trademark and words 'HYGIENIC MERRYTHOUGHT TOYS', usually fixed to the ear or back/shoulder. Following the button was a yellow woven label on the bear.

Printed labels were brought in after the war with 'MERRYTHOUGHT IRONBRIDGE, SHROPS. MADE IN ENGLAND'

In the 1950's the label became wider and carried the words 'MERRYTHOUGHT HYGIENIC TOYS MADE IN ENGLAND', examples of this are rare.

In the 1960's the label was a white printed label, with the added words 'REG'D DESIGN', then in the 1980's the label was printed with yellow colour which was painted onto the label (and tended to rub off) rather than the woven cloth being yellow. In the 1990's yellow woven labels were used.

Tags on the bears were made from card and started in the 1930's in a pale yellow with black type. In the shape of the Merrythought wishbone and the wording 'REG TRADE MARK MERRYTHOUGHT VERYLYTE HYGIENIC TOYS'. In the 1950's the wording on the tag changed to 'REG TRADE MARK MERRYTHOUGHT HYGIENIC TOYS' or with the added variation of 'MADE IN ENGLAND, IRONBRIDGE SHROPSHIRE'. In the 1960's the swing tag changed to blue with the added wording 'PATENT' (and the patent number) or 'PATENT FASTENING' and 'LOCKED IN EYES TEDDYBEAR' or 'No worry over eyes coming out with our Patent Fastening'. In the 1980's the tag became silver and blue metallic finish and in the 1990's used red, white and blue and a picture of the Union Jack.

Tb020. Bill
the burglar
£5 €7

Tb021. Bert
the builder
£5 €7

Tb022. Toby
the tailor
£5 €7

Tb023. Pedro
the pirate
£5 €7

Tb024. Harvey
the huntsman
£5 €7

Tb025. Donald
the doctor
£5 €7

Cheaper than Chips

Tb001. Merrythought Queens
Jubilee Bear No. 1519
£170 €238

Tb002. Russ Berrie No.603/500
Centennial
£90 €126

Tb003. Sandy the sailor
£7 €10

Tb004. Ambrose
the Ambassador
£5 €7

Tb005. Godiva (USA)
chocolatier
£12 €17

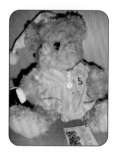

Tb006. Simon
the sleepy head
£5 €7

Tb007. Walter
the wine waiter
£5 €7

Tb008. Royal British Legion
special edition
£40 €56

Tb009. Lionel
the lion tamer
£5 €7

Tb010. Clive
the cashier
£5 €7

Tb011. Ned the
night watchman
£5 €7

Tb012. Dick
the detective
£5 €7

Tb013. Wild Wonder series
Canadian Mountie
£15 €21

Tb014. Philip
the photographer
£5 €7

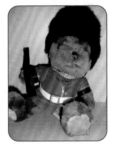

Tb015. Guy
the guardsman
£5 €7

Tb016. Peter
the park keeper
£5 €7

Tb017. Graham
the graduate
£5 €7

Tb018. Stanley
stockbroker
£5 €7

Tb019. Caesar bear
£5 €7

Cheaper than Chips

Tb029. Francis
the florist
£5 €**7**

Tb030. Feddy
the fireman
£5 €**7**

Tb031. Sebastian
the surgeon
£5 €**7**

Tb032. Kim
the karate expert
£5 €**7**

Tb033. Peter
the pilot
£5 €**7**

Tb034. Geoff
the gardener
£5 €**7**

Tb035. Barney
the bellboy
£5 €**7**

Tb036. Derek
the decorator
£5 €**7**

Tb037. Winston
the weight lifter
£5 €**7**

Tb038. Sam the schoolboy
£5 €7

Tb039. Matt
the mechanic
£5 €7

Tb040. Hank
the hot-dog seller
£5 €7

Tb041. Gordon
the golfer
£5 €7

Tb042. Clement
the chef
£5 €7

Tb043. Carl
the conductor
£5 €7

Tb044. Bob
the baseball player
£5 €7

Tb045. Alphonse
the artist
£5 €7

Tb046. Football fan
£8 €11

Tb047. Steve
the station master
£5 €7

Cheaper than Chips

Tb048. Edmond the explorer
£5 €7

Tb049. Furgus the fisherman
£5 €7

Tb050. Bruno the blacksmith
£5 €7

Tb051. Milo the milkman
£5 €7

Tb052. Patrick the postman
£5 €7

Tb053. Basil the butler
£5 €7

Tb054. Santa bear
£10 €14

Tb055. Louis the lumberjack
£5 €7

Tb056. Sidney the scientist
£5 €7

Teddy Bear Collections

The next few pages of teddy bears are from private collections and reflect the enormous growth in this area. Over the past 30 years or so, most people just think of the main producers such as Steiff, Merrythought, Deans and so on.

But this is now a huge cottage industry, and the prices shown over the next few pages are the valuations at either the time of purchase or what the owner now values the bear at. For that reason we do not accept any responsibility

(Continued on Page 185)

Cheaper than Chips

Tb058. Hercules (Lefray) Gwent South Wales **£80 €112**

for any of the prices placed on these items. A great deal of hard work and design has gone into the construction of many of these bears. The materials used are also without equal in the normal market place, but should you be tempted to pay £300 or more for a modern teddy, I'll leave that decision entirely up to you.

Tb059. Hildegard Gunzel (Naseweib) with long scarf **£425 €595**

Tb060. Hildegard Gunzel (Humor King of frogs) **£399 €558**

Tb061. Hadeley Arch bishop of Canterbury by Rowan Williams **£120 €168**

Tb062. Cotswold Raspberry blossom 4/10 **£175 €245**

Tb063. Cotswold Princess Ulac 4/15 by S.J.Bird.& A.Longhi **£175 €245**

Tb064. Cotswold Cherokee 3/100 **£85 €119**

Tb065. Cotswold Shakespeare collection Moth 64/100 **£85 €119**

Tb066. Speedy bears Ali **£40 e56**

Tb067. Billy Buff made by Hazel Slough Lamarr **£50 €70**

Cheaper than Chips

Tb068. Who, Where, What, & Why
213/1000 by D.Canham
£55 €77each

Tb069. Wallace 1/25 by
lD'Lyell Bears
£50 e70

Tb070. Bedspring bears by
Ann Thomas 'Sweet Lilac'
£85 €119

Tb071. Joe Duckworth
Old Australia minx 1/8
£80 €112

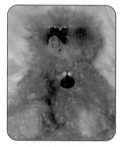

Tb072. Woodland bears 'Pearl'
by Arita; star sign Cancer
£40 €56

Tb073. Woodland bears
'Tigerlilly'; star sign Aries
£40 €56

Tb074. Bosky bear by Diane
'Bosky Panda' 1/10
£80 €112

Tb075. Hooray Henry,
Sloane bears
£40 €56

Tb076. Paddington Gabrielle by
Edward & Shirley Clarkson
£30 €42

Tb077. Barbara-Ann bears
'Waldo' 1/1
£100 €140

Tb078. Barbara-Ann bears
'Wagstaff 1/1
£100 €140

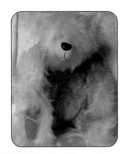

Tb079. April bears by
April Dobson 1/1
£140 €196

Tb080. Navajo bears collection
'Painted Bear'
£60 €84

Tb081. Navajo bears
collection 'Redrock'
£60 €84

Tb082. Navajo bears
collection 'Rainbow'
£60 €84

Tb083. Navajo bears
collection 'Aztec'
£60 €84

Tb084. Something's Bruin by
Jill Hussey 'Puddles'
£30 €42

Tb085. Steiff Polar bears
'Arco'
£100 €140

Tb086. Steiff Micky Mouse
'Fantasia'
£80 €112

Cheaper than Chips

Tb087. Grizzly design 33/333
'Molly Golly'
£50 €70

Tb088. Heike Roland
'Doo Little' 3/25
£80 €112

Tb089. Bears are special collection
'Panda' by Pam Howells
£60 €84

Tb090. Thistledown collection
1/1 'Winkle'
£80 €112

Tb091. Shelly Colbourn collection
'Sandie' 1 of 2
£100 e140

Tb092. Grizzly 'Mirjana Schnepf'
angel bear 28/220
£70 €98

Tb093. F.J. Hannay bears
'Dudley' 3/8
£50 €70

Tb094. Hermann teddy by
Katrin Muller 200/1000
£60 €84

Tb095. Hermann teddy by Gisela
Kaczmarc 'Max' 183/800
£60 €84

Cheaper than Chips

Tb96. Wood-u-like bears 'Fanshaw' moving head
£90 €126

Chad Valley is another very collectable source of toys. Right through the 20th century, as with all the toy companies, they moved quickly with the times. Chad Valley was given the Royal Warrant in 1939. Many of the old cartoons and films are still so popular today because parents continue to pass on or buy toys that were about when they were young. For example Snow White and the Seven Dwarfs, and who has never owned a teddy bear?

Tb97. Tadi 'Garth' with glass eyes
£30 €42

Tb98. Wood-u-like bears 'Jacob 2'moving head
£80 €112

Tb99. Steiner by Angie Zattl 'Arabella' 1/14
£70 €98

Tb100. Futch bears 'Tuppence' 2/2
£50 €70

Tb101. Futch bears 'Scarlet'
£50 €70

Tb102. Nursery bears 'Baby boy' by Linda Henry
£120 €168

Tb103. Milhouse bears 'Chocice' 3/5
£50 €70

Tb104. Lillian Frigg bears 'Elijah'
£100 €140

Tb105. Deans 'Truffles' by Janet Clark 116/1500
£100 €140

Cheaper than Chips

Tb110. Barton Creek 'Aurora' green, 'Leah' purple
£40 €56 each

Tb107. Deans 'Raspberry Sorbet' by Janet Clark 224/500
£170 €238

Tb108. Georgina Vienna memories in lace 'Jasmine' 3/50
£50 €70

Tb109. Robin Reeve 'Melissa' Millennium Edition. 47/500
£40 €56

Tb106. Deans 'Jack Junior' 143/500
£130 €182

Tb111. Lillian Trigg 'Sybil' born 17/4/02 @21.02
£60 €84

Tb112. Puzzle bears by Anita Weller no. LT209 & LT440
£70 €90 each

Tb113. Turner's Teddies 'Bugsy' by Sue Turner
£50 €70

Tb114. Sue Shillingford 'Sybil' in cup 1/1
£100 €140

Tb115. Maryke bears
'LinLin' 4/10
£50 €70

Tb116. Debra Lawrence
'Lloyd' 1/1
£80 €112

Tb117. Grizzly bears
'Margaret' 12/444
£75 €105

Tb118. Send r fur message bears
by Fat Dallys 'Pyjamas'
£35 €49

Tb119. Send r fur message
bears by Fat Dallys
'Rucksack' **£35 €49**

Tb120. BIG ger bears by
Deb.Canham 'Whatever'
81/200 **£70 €98**

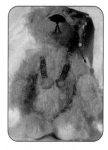

Tb121. BIG ger bears by
Deb.Canham 'So what'
115/200 **£70 €98**

Tb122. Bear hugs by
Bev.McNab 'Sand'
£80 €112

Tb123. Bear hugs by
Bev.McNab
£80 €112

Tb124. Beanie bears 'Tia' by
Janette Wilson, material
Alpaca. 4/8 **£70 €90**

Cheaper than Chips

Tb125. Billy Buff 'Ben' D.o.b
29/12/98 double jointed head
£100 €140

Tb126. Cherished teddies
'John'
£30 €42

Tb127. Cherished teddies
'Jennifer'
£30 €42

Tb128. Cherished teddies
4800 Ltd edition
£30 €42

Tb129. Ganz cottage
collectibles 'Doris'
£30 €42

Tb130. Ganz
'Candy'
£20 €28

Tb131. Ganz
'Summer'
£20 €28

Tb132. Ganz
'Fall'
£20 €28

Tb133. Ganz
'Tic, Tac, & Toe'
£20 €28 each

Tb134. Bow-wood bears
'Tasha' by Jan.Draper
£45 €63

Tb135. Clemens Spieltiere
'Willy Windig' 23/599
£50 €70

Tb136. Bear bits 'Vostok' 9/25
double-jointed head
£100 €140

Tb137. Ganz cottage collectable
TD Fearless & Cinders
£160 €224 pair

Tb138. Maryke bears
'Roderick' 1/1
£90 €126

Tb139. Ganz 'Celia'
1374/2400
£100 €140

Tb140. Grizley growls
'Matthew' 95/333 by
R.Geary **£80 €112**

Tb141. Orkid bears growls
'Gwydion'
Michelle Nicolls
£70 €90

Tb142. Deans 'Pooh & Piglet'
£180 €252 pair

Tb143. Deans
'Eeyore' 217/3000
£90 €126

Cheaper than Chips

Tb145. Herman minatures
all 175/300
£30 €42 each

Tb144. Deans '
Chinese gooseberry'
32/250 **£60 €84**

Tb146. Quarrington 'Bob'
by June Whitehead
£50 €70

Tb147. Grizzly 'Peanut butter'
by Susan Geary 235/444
£80 €112

Tb148. Gallery bear No1612
by Debbie Henretty
£30 €42

Tb026. Colin
the captain
£5 €7

Tb027. Tim
the tennis player
£5 €7

Tb028. Henry
the hiker **£5 €7**

NC77. Silver-plated
egg & spoon tray
£14 €19

NC78. Limoges
china box
£16 €22

NC80. Miniature Limoges
plate 70mm
£4 €6

NC81. Miniature Limoges
plate 50mm
£5 €7

NC82. Miniature Limoges
plate 50mm
£5 €7

NC83. Limoges box
125mm
£26 €37

NC84. Limoges
pot & lid
£25 €35

NC85. Royal Doulton
stoneware jug
£78 €109

NC86. Adams plate
1930's
£7 €10

NC87. Chessel pottery
vase
£16 €22

Cheaper than Chips

1a. Pair of military amulets **£30 €42**

2a. A 19c. brass theodolite **£140 €196**

3a. Set of postal scales **£25 €35**

4a. Three turned wooden boxes **£25 €35**

5a. Brass & copper calendar 1941-95 **£25 €35**

6a. Two policemens' truncheons **£30 €42**

7a. Car badge 'Spirit of the wind' **£50 €70**

8a. Brass carriage clock **£80 €112**

9a. 19c. fruitwood spinning wheel **£70 €98**

10a. 19c. ornate gilt/brass mantel clock **£140 €196**

Storage

No-body can predict which items available today will one day become valuable. Take care when packing items away in the attic or garage to ensure they are secure and dry.

11a. Gilt metal mantle clock **£50 €70**

12a. Brass theodolite **£50 €70**

13a. Two carved Japanese figures **£40 €56**

14a. Royal Automobile Club badge **£20 €28**

15a. Slate & marble mantle clock **£80 €112**

16a. Old bolt action lock **£30 €42**

17a. Oriental white glazed terracotta piece **£40 €56**

18a. Carved soapstone dragon **£40 €56**

19a. Edwardian walnut table top cabinet **£60 €84**

20a. Collection of tennis memorabilia **£30 e42**

21a. Early 20c battery lantern **£30 e42**

Cheaper than Chips

22a. Two brass warming trivets
£15 e21

23a. 1930's crossbanded walnut clock
£50 e70

24a. Flintlock pistol & powder flask
£100 e140

25a. 1950's/60's Doll
£50 e70

26a. Dolly circa 1970's
£40 e56

27a. 2 large dollies
£70 e98

28a. 3 soft toy dollies
£70 e98

29a. Late 19c. vehicle lamp
£30 e42

30a. Wall clock & barometer
£45 e63

31a. Soft toy tiger
£25 e35

Composite Dolls...

...date back thousands of years, and are very collectable indeed. They are relatively rare, but many fine examples have been produced over the last 100 years or so that do come to market. They vary in their construction wildly from painted wood, to clay porcelain or wax to name but a few. Painted porcelain and bisque models are the most sought after by today's collectors, and there are a good few around, even models from the 1950's & 60's can be worth hundreds of pounds. So never walk past one looking a bit sad and dirty in a box without at least checking it out.

32a. Conway cameras
£40 €56

33a. Edwardian ink stand
£45 €63

34a. Bing horizontal
steam engine
£50 €70

35a. Musical
squeeze box
£70 €98

36a. Boxed 19c.
Sextant
£100 €140

37a. Piano action
Italian accordion
£40 €56

38a. Trumpet in a case
£50 €70

39a. North American
Indian head-dress
£30 €42

42a. Charlie Chaplin
character jug
£20 e28

40a. Violin in its case
£70 €98

41a. Wedgewood
part dinner service
£50 €70

43a. 2 Decanters
& stoppers
£20 928

Cheaper than Chips

386. A blue and white vegetable tureen and three plates
£30 €42

387. American Revolution commemorative plate
£25 €35

388. Bretby car
£35 €49

389. A Denby vase
£40 €56

391. Part of picture 390.

394. A Moorcroft vase
£190 €266

390. Royal Copenhagen part dinner service **£70 €98**

392. A cut glass bowl on stand **£50 €70**

393. A blue and white faience jug **£50 €70**

Bretby Pottery

Established in the 1880's, Bretby Pottery has produce many novelty items throughout its history and the picture 388 is a reasonable example of this. They also made a series of half-size figures, primarily of children. The pottery closed early in the 20th Century.

44a. Sylvac character jug
'George Bernard Shaw'
£30 €42

45a. China comport,
Indian tree pattern
£20 €28

46a. Pair of Carnival
glass dishes
£40 €56

47a. Royal Winton
bowl & cover
£20 €28

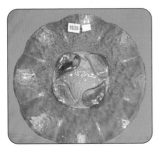

48a. Ornate green glass dish
£40 €56

49a. Set Royal Worcester
ramekins **£15 €21**

50a. 2 blue & white
dishes
£40 €56

51a. 3 Motto ware
pieces
£20 €28

52a. Late 20c Wedgewood
tea-set **£30 €42**

53a. Royal Doulton jug
Sir Francis Drake
£65 €91

Cheaper than Chips

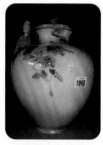

54a. Royal Doulton green glazed vase **£100 €140**

55a. Moorcroft vase **£120 €168**

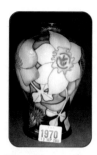

56a. Moorcroft vase **£150 €210**

58a. Royal Worcester commemorative plate **£40 €56**

57a. Moorcroft vase **£220 €308**

59a. Moorcroft vase **£180 €252**

60a. Moorcroft plate **£60 €84**

61a. 2 Continental porcelain figures **£30 €42**

62a. Royal Worcester gilt coffee set **£40 €56**

63a. Coalport figure of Romeo & Juliet **£40 €56**

64a. Royal Doulton jug **£45 €63**

HY25. Hand worked brass Indian beaker **£10 €14**

66a. Pair Staffordshire
dogs **£100** €**140**

67a. Collection of china
pots/vases/bowls
£40 €**56**

68a. Two Bing vertical
steam engines
£120 €**168**

69a. Leather
cannon-ball carrier
£80 €**112**

70a. Portmerion
Tureen & cover
£80 €**112**

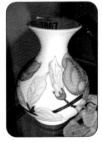

71a. Moorcroft
vase
£120 €**168**

72a. Moorcroft
tea-pot
£240 €**336**

73a. Small Moorcroft
dish **£40** €**56**

74a. Moorcroft saucer
£35 €**49**

75a. Royal Doulton character
jug Beefeater
£50 €**70**

Cheaper than Chips

76a. Moorcroft
dish
£60 €84

77a. Poole pottery
vase
£40 €56

78a. Small
Moorcroft vase
£30 €42

81a. Collection of
Hummel & Geobel
figures **£160 €224**

79a. Coalport
figure
£30 €42

80a. Royal Doulton
figure 'Elaine'
£90 €126

82a. Small Moorcroft
vase **£60 €84**

83a. Wedgewood blue
jasper ware clock
£30 €42

84a. Lladro figure &
Continental figure
£45+£15 €63+21

85a. Beswick figure
'Mrs Tiggywinkle'
£45 €63

86a. Moorcroft
vase
£100 €140

87a. 19c. Oriental bronze
temple censor
£30 €42

LM20. Royal Doulton miniature. 'Pretty as a picture' **£80 €112**

396. A Carlton ware shell cruet set **£30 €42**

397. Three Wedgewood Christmas plates **£35 €49**

398. Three Wedgewood Edward VIII commemorative plates **£40 €56**

399. Royal Doulton slaters patent jar **£35 €49**

400. A carnival glass dish **£30 €42**

LM49. The little owl **£5 €7**

LM22. Royal Doulton fig. of the year 2003 'Elizabeth' **£140 €196**

LM23. Royal Doulton fig. of the year 1999 'Lauren' **£150 €210**

LM24. Royal Doulton fig. of the year 1998 'Rebecca' **£160 €224**

Cheaper than Chips

LM25. Royal Doulton classics 'Emma' **£80 €112**

412. A Poole pottery dish **£60 €84**

408. A Carlton ware dish **£20 €28**

407. Wedgewood Blue Jasper ware Xmas plates **£100 €140**

409. Royal Doulton Norfolk pattern part tea service **£90 €126**

410. A majolica cake comport **£15 €21**

411. A Shelley bowl **£25 €35**

LM26. Royal Doulton fig. 2001 'Melissa' **£140 €196**

413. A Shelley bowl **£20 €28**

Shed some Light

Taking an antique into the light of day can be difficult or impossible. The alternative is to bring a light of your own to get a better look at the item. This may reveal imperfections, which may not stop you from making the purchase but may help you in deciding a fair price. Of course, if there is no power source available on site you will need a battery-operated, portable light.

Having a closer look may also reveal subtle differences in the colour of wood or tell you if wood furniture has been restored. Light can also show you whether the back of a painting has been

(Continued on Page 207.)

relined, a restoration technique that detracts from a pieces worth.

Other handy hints are to take a small magnifying glass to look at intricate details and a mirror to view the back of larger pieces you are unable to get behind. You may find a notebook handy and perhaps a reference book to look up anything you are not sure of.

414. A pair of vases with covers **£50** **€70**

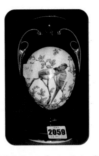

415. Royal Doulton John Barleycorn character mug **£50** **€70**

416. Transfer printed vase **£20** **€28**

417. Wedgewood coffee pot **£20** **€28**

418. Three pieces of White Friars glass **£50** **€70**

LM01. The Leonardo collection 'Antique shop' **£15** **€21**

LM02. Beatrix Potter 'Ginger & Pickles shop' **£15** **€21**

421. T.G. Green & Co. salt pot **£30** **€42**

422. Satsuma bell jar and cover **£80** **€112**

427. Royal Doulton miniature character jug 'Robin Hood' **£30** **€43**

Cheaper than Chips

423. Meissen plate
£30 €42

424. Base of picture 423
Meissen mark

425. Two Copeland Spode butter
and preserve pots **£30 €42**

LM03. The Leonardo collection
'Dodgems' tea pot
£10 €14

428. Continental pottery vase
and cover **£30 e42**

429. Pottery bowl
£20 €28

430. Wedgewood blue and
white bowl **£20 €28**

431. Cut glass tray
£20 €28

432.Coloured glass fish
£10 €14

433.Coloured glass clown
£10 €14

435.Three graduated Staffordshire
salt glazed jugs £80 €112

438.Continental handled
oval bowl £60 €84

434.Coloured glass
vase £10 €14

436.Oriental figure of
Kuan Yin £30 €42

437.Pair of Royal Doulton
vases £80 €112

441.Trio of tea/cup saucer
and plate £30 €42

439.Two flow blue tureens and
covers £80 €112

340.Pair of Cloisonné
plates £40 €56

Cheaper than Chips

442. Crown Staffordshire tea-set **£30 €42**

443.T.G. Green & Co. cube mini teapot **£30 €42**

444. Royal Doulton and Rixs patent vase **£80 €112**

445. Royal Doulton Copenhagen figure, Puma **£150 €210**

446.19c. Staffordshire dog **£80 €12**

447. Set Meissen dishes **£60 €84**

448. Beswick figure Lady Hunting **£70 €98**

449. Two oriental vases **£25 €35**

450. Royal Doulton Bunnykins nursery bowl **£20 €28**

Selling Treasured Possessions

If you plan to sell an item which has perhaps been in your family for a long time or that you know to be valuable there are a few handy hints to remember.

In getting a price guide right get more than one opinion but remember if you are talking to the owner of an antiques store who is a potential buyer they may have a vested interest in the price they give you. However, this does not mean the price is not fair. It is worth bearing in mind that a

(Continued on Page 211)

91a. Royal Doulton figure 'The Judge'
£85 €119

dealer may be able to sell the item for a higher value than that you will obtain on a private sale.

It is worth remembering also that the piece may be more valuable than the price given to you due to your personal interest, if that is the case and you don't need to sell - hold on to it and you never know the market may change.

88a. Carved wooden figures & stoppers
£30 €42

89a. 2 Mother of pearl & silver bowls
£40 €56

90a. 3 old cameras
£10 €14

92a. Five commemorative plates **£15 €21**

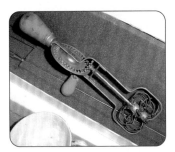

94a. Old food whisk
£5 €7

95a. Moorland bowl **£40 €56**

93a. Lorna Bailey novelty inkwell
£40 €56

96a. Wedgewood plates 'London street sellers'
£30 €42

97a. Moorland crocus pattern jug
£25 €35

Cheaper than Chips

98a. Pair Lorna Bailey novelty peppers
£40 **€56**

99a. Chelsea / Moorland tea-pot
£40 **€56**

100a. Moorland tea-pot
£40 **€56**

101a. Lorna Bailey House-Path jug
£55 **€77**

102a. Poole pottery vase
£20 **€28**

103a. Masons Ironstone serving tray
£40 **€56**

104a. Lorna Bailey storage jar
£75 **€105**

105a. Stationery box
£50 **€70**

106a. Poole pottery vase
£20 **€28**

107a. Masons tureen & cover **£40** **€56**

108a. Jersey creamer by T.G. Green
£30 **€42**

109a. Lorna Bailey jug astral pattern
£60 **€84**

T. G. Green

Founded in 1864 in Church Gresley near Burton on Trent mainly producing general household items. Best known of these were 'Cornish Kitchen Ware' also a very sturdy range of earthenwares and stonewares, right up there for the collector of kitchenalia. Blue and white Cornish kitchen ware is a favourite still in production today.

111a. Poole baluster vase
£40 €56

110a. Poole Dolphin figure
£25 €35

112a. Box of collectable bottles
£25 €35

113a. G.P.O. telephone cash slot box
£45 €63

116a. Sylvac vase
£5 €7

114a. Metal sugar bowl with covers & scoop
£10 €14

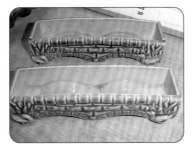

115a. Two Wade trinket items
£10 €14

HY26. Polish tin teapot
£5 €7

118a. Old toaster. Art deco
£20 €28

119a. Collection of boxed Star Trek toys
£25 €35

120a. Clarice Cliff moulded tureen & plates
£20 €28

Cheaper than Chips

122a. Drum set
£40 €56

121a. Set of scales & weights
£20 €28

124a. Public house
display case
£10 €14

125a. Pair Wade
tortoises
£10 €14

126a. Opera glasses
£5 €7

127a. Opera glasses
£5 €7

128a. Modern
opera glasses
£5 €7

129a. Old set of binoculars
£5 €7

130a. Hand held 70's
16mm cine camera
£10 €14

Opera Glasses

There are many different types of opera glasses out there to collect. It would be difficult to walk round a medium size car boot sale without seeing at least 5 pairs, priced from a few pounds up to hundreds of pounds.

123a. Victorian
commode
£30 €42

Cheaper than Chips

454. Cake plate **£15** €21

Reserve Price

You may if you wish reserve a sale price on your items at auction. This means that although you expect a sale value such as £120, you would be prepared to accept your reserve price of £90 - this ensures the item is not sold for lower than this price. In some cases auctions will purchase the item at the reserve price, judging that the item will sell for more at a later date. The terminology for this is 'bought in'.

451. Flight Barr and Barr bowl **£30** €42

457. Early fire extinguisher **£40** €56

453. Royal Doulton tea-set **£60** €84

455. Bridgewood Art Deco part dinner service **£50** €70

452. Copeland Spode tureen stand and three dishes **£50** €70

456. Glass domed case of stuffed birds **£80** €112

458. 1950 dolly **£20** €28

459. Early 20c. dressed dolly **£50** €70

460. Early 20c. dressed dolly **£60** €84

461. Twyford teddy **£40** €56

Cheaper than Chips

131a. Public house display case
£10 €14

132a. Underwood typewriter
£5 €7

133a. Georgian boot scraper
£100 €140

137a. Wind-up wall clock
£15 €21

134a. Mid 20c. enamelled colander
£2 €3

135a. Enamelled flour bin
£4 €6

136a. Enamelled bread bin
£5 €7

138a. Modern wood burner
£20 €28

139a. Decorative cast wood burner
£40 €56

140a. Modern wood burner
£30 €42

141a. 3 small Belfast sinks
£30 e42

Kitchenalia

Kitchenalia is probably the most impressive area of growth in the car boot and antique market. Any new collector could soon build a very impressive collection, from hand tools such as rolling pins and storage bins right up to some very collectable china and porcelain. Even items as recent as the 1970's and 1980's are becoming very collectable. If you are considering taking up carbooting on a regular

(Continued on Page 217)

basis, then this is a range of products that will keep people visiting your stall regularly. Your own kitchen or maybe your parent's one, or any auction will provide you with a good range of products. Small preserve pots, enamelled bins and colanders which at auction are usually sold in boxes as lots with as many as 10 to 50 pieces of kitchen ware going under the hammer for as little as £5.

High quality items such as tureens and meat serving dishes will always sell well as single items. So often a single serving dish could be worth chasing at auction especially if it's in a box of say 10 other items. Kitchenalia has such a large following you will seldom end up with unsold items.

Many famous names have produced kitchenalia over the last 150 years or so. I'm not suggesting for a second that you will purchase a box of kitchenalia full of Royal Doulton, Royal Worcester or the like at auction for £5, but you might well find things like rolling pins, mixing bowls, preserve jars, coloured glass bottles or even single items of silver such as spoons, carving knives or serving utensils.

Mass produced items which have become unpopular with the modern household such as jelly and aspic moulds or commemorative items have been thrown out by the thousand over the last 30 years or so or have just been shoved to the back of a cupboard or attic. Our parents were just as likely to have a best china service or crockery items that had little use, as we do today. Now is the time to sort them out. I could easily list 50 or more makers as collectable today, and over the past 20 years of buying and selling at auction houses I have nearly always made a good profit on items from the kitchen.

Inherited items, or items with sentimental associations usually included favourite serving dishes and tureens, but I would like to say that many of these items are offar too good quality, or too collectable in today's market to now be ignored and stored away.

But please do your research before you tear off to the car boot sale with great great grandmother's Mason Ironstone dinner service, hoping to raise enough for a pub lunch on the way home as that's all you might get!

Do not be put off if pieces are chipped or cracked, as one cracked plate in a set of say 8, or a chipped tureen for example, will still be of value to the collector who can easily replace a single item, as the pattern or design is usually recorded on the back or bottom of the piece.

Better still, plan ahead and search the internet or bric-a-brac shops for single items. Collectors shop will look out for single items for you if you just give them the details of the piece you are looking for and a telephone number. They are normally happy to track down a piece for you but be prepared to be patient and to pay a premium for this service. Offset this though against the auction price of a full set of good condition crockery and you can command a high price.

143a. Brass candle holder
& snub
£20 €28

142a. 2 Ships lanterns
£100 €140

Cheaper than Chips

560. Victorian ebonised smoking cabinet **£80** €**112**

561. Inside of picture 560.

564. Victorian magic lantern **£150** €**210**

562. Tin-plated fire engine **£40** €**56**

565. Victorian brass fire irons **£30** €**42**

566. Wooden goose **£20** €**28**

567. Victorian copper coal scuttle **£30** €**42**

568. Victorian brass jardiniere **£20** €**28**

569. Head plaque **£40** €**56**

Cheaper than Chips

H3. Jane Asher Ltd. Edition china box **£12** €**17**

H1. Hardwood & brass coal box **£28** €**39**

H2. 4711 perfume bottle c1960 **£5** €**7**

H4. German porceline candle display piece **£46** €**64**

H6. Precision scales by Baird & Tatlock **£85** €**119**

H5. Heavy blue glass lidded pot **£20** €**28**

H8. Carved hardwood pot holders **£20** €**28**

H7. Odd pair of wall lights **£20** €**28**

H9. Limoges tureen **£38** €**53**

H10. Royal Venton ware preserve pot **£8** €**11**

H12. Selection of lead farm animals from **£2** €**3**

Cheaper than Chips

H11. Copper bed warming pan **£68 €95**

H13. Victorian flat iron **£8 €11**

H14. A Dean's soft toy **£12 €17**

H15. Set of Salter household scales **£15 €21**

H16. Honiton ware vases from **£8 €11**

H17. Pair of Radford vases 150mm each **£8 €11**

H19. Hobnail design blue vase **£10 €14**

H18. Carnival glass bowl **£13 €18**

H20. Pair of 'Cherub' china wall pockets **£38 €53**

H21. Mid 20c. 'Shirley Temple' doll **£60 €84**

Honiton

Honiton art potteries were established in Honiton Devon from 1881. The light and creamy texture of the wares, although mass produced, are collectable in today's market. The flowery and plain designs soon found favour in the early 20th century; look out for early pieces marked the Honiton Lace Art Pottery Co. This early mark was registered in 1915 but changed to just 'Honiton Pottery Devon' in 1947.

H22. Pair modern
'Wizard' book ends
£20 €28

H23. Pair iron Horse
door stops
£30 €42

H26. Victorian gothic
style clock
£80 €112

H29. Minton, Edward VIII
coronation cup
£20 €28

H24. Oriental decorated
tea caddie
£32 €45

H25. Inside view of
picture H24.

H28. 60's Pepsi
water jug
£5 €7

H27. Art deco style onyx mantel clock
£120 €168

H30. George V1 & Elizabeth
coronation cup 1937,
£12 €17

H32. Continental
2 litre petrol tin
£5 €7

Cheaper than Chips

H31. Coalport
Charles & Diana plate
£30 €42

H33. Modern black &
white panda toy
£3 €4

H34. Queen Elizabeth II
silver jubilee mug
1977, **£4 €5**

H35. Queen Elizabeth II
silver jubilee mug
1977, **£4 €5**

H36. Queen Elizabeth II
silver jubilee mug
1977, **£4 €5**

H37. Queen Elizabeth II
silver jubilee mug
1977, **£4 €5**

H38. The coronation of
Elizabeth II 1953
£5 €7

H39. The coronation of
Elizabeth II 1953
£5 €7

H40. Engagement mug
Prince Charles & Diana
£3 €4

H41. Engagement mug
Prince Andrew & Sarah
£4 €5

Commemorative Ware...

...over the last 100 years or so has become big business, but the art of making any real cash with these items is to be very selective. Unfortunately most were made by the thousand to fuel the market of the time, and their quality was usually poor. As you can see from the above they will tick over to the collector of commemorative items, and will usually go. But try to keep your search to well known makers such as Royal Worcester, Royal Doulton or Coalport.

H50. 3 brass spirit
measures
£18 €25

H42. Queen Elizabeth II
silver jubilee mug
£3 €4

H43. Coronation mug George VI
& Elizabeth, 1937,
£7 €10

H44. Marriage of
Prince Charles to Lady Diana
1981, **£5 €7**

H45. Two enamel casserole pots
£8 €11

H46. Continental
coffee grinder
£10 €14

H47. Bottle brut
aftershave 1980's
£5 €7

H48. Victorian copper
measure jug
£5 €7

H49. Porcelain
mantel clock
£20 €28

H51. Lamp bases from
the Celtic pottery
£32 €45

Cheaper than Chips

H53. A bean slicer "Alsops" **£25 €35**

H54. 5 miniature copper sauce pans **£10 €14**

H52. 1970's plastic Homepride flourman **£10 €14**

H55. Model wood kit of Cutty Sark **£20 €28**

H57. Tobacco & sweet tins **£1 €2**

H58. Tobacco & sweet tins **£1 €2**

H59. Tobacco & sweet tins **£1 €2**

H56. Model wood kit of The Fragata **£20 €28**

Tins

Every garage or shed in the country is certain to have old tins in them used for storage of nails, pins, nuts, bolts and the like, but there is a healthy market for the collector of these items. Some well known companies have, over the last 100 years, turned to the humble tin to market their products. Some early makers such as Oxo and Cadbury's are sought after.

H60. Tobacco & sweet tins
£1 €2

H61. Tobacco & sweet tins
£1 €2

H62. Cigarette tin £1 €2

H64. Tobacco & sweet tins £1
€2

H66. Collection of old bottles
£2 €3

H63. Tobacco tins
£1 €2

H65. Collection of old bottles
£2 €3

H67. Braimes double-sided oil
cans pair £5 €7

Cheaper than Chips

H69. Set of meat or cheese scales enamelled tray
£10 €14

H70. Set of shop scales for vegetables
£8 €11

H71. Modern hand painted pot & cover
£5 €7

H72. Wade Bells Scotch whisky bottle
£10 €14

H73. Stone glaze flagons 'Aylesbury' ginger beer
£22 €31

H74. Selection of servants downstairs bells
£15 €21 each

H77. Restored Train warning light
£30 €42

H75. Selection of servants bells
£15 €21 each

H68. 2 Smarties egg cups
£4 €6

Myott Pottery

Myott first started production in 1898 at Stoke producing tableware, the word Stoke appearing on the back before 1903. Many traditional country scenes were transfer printed onto earthenware and porcelain plates and dishes.

The company was renamed Myott-Meakin in 1977. Ever popular with plate collectors for decoration as wall hung plates or for dressers. Larger pieces or sets are very sought after so pick the odd single piece up if you come across one.

H76. Cast enamel & brass scales **£10** €14

H78. 60's Warwick castle
biscuit tin
£8 €11

H79. Electric radio
by Mullard
£25 €35

H80. 4 Charles Dickens
scene plates
£12 €17

H81. Old electric radio
£20 €28

H82. Carved hardwood
Chinese lantern
£85 €119

H83. Front grill from
MG .sports car
£50 €70

H84. Large Tonka tipper
truck c1980?
£12 €17

H85. Myott pottery
'The chase'
£6 €8

H86. Myott pottery,
'Country life' series
£6 €8

H87. Myott, 'Ccountry
life' scene bowl
£8 €11

Cheaper than Chips

H89. 3 modern stone glaze pots
£10 €14

H90. Ferguson electric radio
£10 €14

H91. GEC.Electric radio
£12 €17

H92. Pink Panther foam doll
£8 €11

H93. Black & white cat £6 €8

H96. Cast iron cooking pot
£8 €11

H94. Two brass plumbers blow torches
£8 €11 each

H95. Two brass blow torches
£8 €11 each

H88. Smith Premier typewriter no.10,
£10 €14

Toys

Personally speaking, old toys, from as early as the 1970's, I see as being the one growth area for the carbooter who is looking for a tidy sum from a good spring clean, as few complete or undamaged pieces come onto the market. Complete, boxed working toys fetch big money, but don't worry if you were normal and threw the boxes out and played with the toys as virtually all toys from the 1940's to the 1970's have a good collectors' market, so it is time to give them up.

H97. Glazed stoneware preserves jar
£5 €7

H98. Child's Chad valley spinning top
£6 €8

H99. Cut glass dressing table box
£35 €49

H100. Brass & wood stationary box
£60 €84

H101. Inside picture box H100.

H102. Inlaid desk top writing slope
£70 €98

H103. Open picture of writing slope pic.102.

H104. Dallas child's 10 note xylophone
£20 €28

H105. Booths blue & white tureen A/F
£8 €11

H106. Merrythought bears c1980
£40 €56

Cheaper than Chips

H108. Brass & cast handle saucepan
£15 €21

H109. Liston luxor ware c1920
£10 €14

H110. 19c Flintlock pistol
£250 €350

H111. Stanley no79 double sided rebate tool
£36 €50

H112. African dagger ivory/brass/leather sheath
£8 €11

H107. Carlton ware leaf dish
£7 €10

Tools

Tools are also a good money raiser at any car boot sale. All of us have a selection of modern drills, sanders, saws. planes and the like, but the modern electric items that have come onto the market have made many thousands of old tools redundant. Many of these tools have been produced to the highest standards of the time using the best materials for strength. So if you are clearing the shed or garage soon - take care!!

H113. 3" silver plate cigarette case
£32 €45

H115. Early 20c rifle telescopic sight
£35 €49

H117. Old box camera
£20 €28

H114. Brass 19c gunpowder flask
£35 €49

H116. 19c shot charger measure
£35 €49

H118. Ambassador deluxe light meter
£10 €14

H119. Baby Zeiss 16 on 120 camera
£30 €42

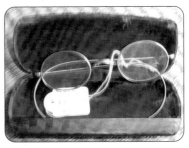

H120. Pair gold rim spectacles in original box
£10 €14

Cheaper than Chips

H121. Metric thread gauge
£10 €14

H123. Marples ebony mortice gauge
£38 €53

H124. 20c Miniature
pocket telescope
£16 €22

H125. Small German travelling
alarm clock c1920
£50 €70

H126. Kodapod?
USA 1915
£10 €14

H127. 2 Silver match holders
£20 €28

H122. Milbro early 20c
fishing reel
£25 €35

H128. Lead crystal
paperweight inkwell
£18 €25

H129. 1970's
Fozzie bear
£5 €7

H130. Brass crab inkwell
£12 €17

H131. Hardwood
letter rack
£10 €14

H132. Beefeater plastic
ice bucket
£25 €35

H133. Kaye's patent oil cans
£10 €14

H134. Pair brass pendulum
clock weights
£22 €30

H135. Eaton Sun patent
fishing reel
£10 €14

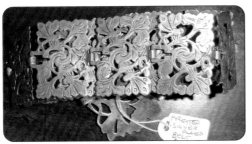

H136. Fret work silver plated belt
£45 €63

H137. Royal Worcester jug
c1880 willow pattern
£80 €112

H138. Victorian chest lock
£18 €25

Cheaper than Chips

H139. Zorfi camera
in leather case
£55 €77

H140. Agfa Karat
Compur camera
£26 €36

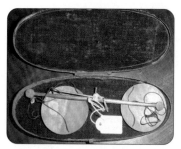

H141. 20c Medical
scales in case
£20 €28

H142. Voigtlander
Vito B camera
£25 €35

H144. Royal Worcester
figure 'First Dance'
A/F **£60 €84**

H146. Kodak Pronto-LK
(German) camera
£15 €21

H145. Mark of base of
Royal Worcester
pic.144.

H143. Royal Doulton George V
& Queen Mary dish
£20 e28

H147. Victorian cast
pan warmer
£25 €35

H148. RAF issue mug
£8 €11

H149. Small cut glass
rose bowl
£6 €8

H150. 6" cut glass
rose bowl
£8 €11

H151. Silver-plated
pot planter
£16 €22

H152. 4 framed
silk pictures
£16 €22

H153. Collection of
blue glass bottles
£5 €7 each

H154. 2 Brass framed pictures
£32 €45

H155. Black & White
whisky wall plaque
£38 €53

H156. Radford
table ware
£30 €42

H157. Transfer printed
Masons water jug
£6 €8

H158. Victorian
clothes pegs
£2 €3 each

Cheaper than Chips

H160. Staffordshire
Spaniel
£16 €22

H161. Tortoise brass and
glass nightlight
£25 €35

H162. Pair glass crystal
candlesticks
£45 €63

H163. Queen Elizabeth II Coronation dishes
£5 €7 each

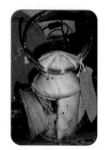

H164. Train front
warning light
£22 €31

H165. Train front
warning light
£22 €31

H166. Train red rear warning
light **£40 €56**

H159. Wade porcelain log
£6 €8

H168. Car horn c1920s
Brass & rubber A/F
£10 €14

Ship & Train Warning Lights

You will often see these items at the auction house, especially around coastal regions. They are well constructed and built to withstand the toughest of weather conditions, strapped to a train or ship, these lamps have truly earned a place on the collectors' list of 'must have' items. Once restored (normally a good clean and a lick of paint) they are finding their way into many thousands of gardens and many are still working, but if not, a candle will supply a warm glow!

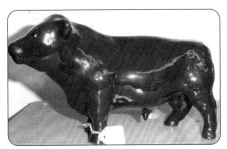

H167. China Bull **£8** €**11**

H169. Brass & glass
tortoise nightlight
£22 €**31**

H170. Continental wall hung
coffee grinder
£22 €**31**

H172. Coffee bean roaster
£12 €**17**

H173. Spannungs
volt regulator
£15 €**21**

H174. Victorian iron hot plate
slips inside
£12 €**17**

H171. 2 Enamel
saucepans/steamers
£10 €**14**

H175. Shelly dish A/F
£6 €**8**

H176. Makin
lady golfer teddy
£5 €**7**

H177. Brass blow lamp
£8 €**11**

H178. Oak & tapestry
fire screen
£18 €25

H180. Spice or
coffee grinder
£8 €11

H181. Drinks barrel decanter
& 6 glass tumblers
£10 €14

H182. Boy Scout motive,
copper bed warming
pan **£25 €35**

H179. Chrome & tapestry
fire screen
£28 €39

H183. Brass munitions
shell case planter
£40 €56

H184. Oak barrel on stand
£25 €35

H185. 1950/60's
meat mince
£3 €4

H186. 1960's Hack
battery radio
£20 €28

H187. Original
water pump
£40 €56

BESWICK POTTERY 1894 TO PRESENT DAY

In the early years Beswick manufactured mainly 'useable pottery', toilet seats, table wares, tea services, vases and flowerpots. This style of manufacture ensured the prosperity of the factory through the First World War.

In the 1930's the emphasis carried from the functional over to novelty pottery. This is the area for which Beswick is best known; the naturalistic study of animals, which were initially the mantelpiece ornaments of the traditional Staffordshire type.

Jim Greaves the decorating manager at the time developed the novelty pottery. The company also used freelance modellers; a Miss Greaves developed one of the first series of 12 children.

In 1939 the company employed their first resident modeller, Arthur Gredington, who by producing around 400 models made a major contribution to the success of the company. His first major project was a copy of 12 figures first done by Nun Maria Innocentia Hummel in Germany. These Hummel 'look alikes' are now as desirable as the originals, if not more!

Other models covered a wide range of figures, including race horses, wild animals, farm breeds, championship dogs and then went on to initiate the Beatrix Potter series, also Snow White and the Seven Dwarfs.

Post war the factory produced a range of patriotic figures (Churchill) inspired by the war.

Another series produced was that of a group of four fairies, which is very hard to find today, along with a clown and a jester.

The post war figures were usually wearing contemporary dress, i.e. a butcher boy, a hiker and a sportsman.

Jan Granoska, from Eastern Europe designed some of the finest human figures. These included a range of girls of different nationalities in traditional costume, such as the Italian Girl and Swedish Girl doing their Country's national dance or interacting with farm animals. Granoska also famously produced the Peter Pan and Pinocchio series.

In the 1940's Gredington showed his prowess for the equestrian theme, firstly modelling the Rearing Horseman, the last he modelled was Arkle being ridden by Pat Taffe.

After Gredington retired, Albert Hallam kept up the tradition of the famous race horse models, with famous jockeys riding them, for instance Nijinksy with Lester Piggott riding.

Graham Tongue did the 'Blues and Royals' series.

Beswick steered away from the more traditional 'lady' themes of Doulton, with one rare exception 'Lady in Ballgown' which was produced for just one year. The company preferred the more 'humorous' lines, such as 'The Road Gang' and 'Bedtime Chorus' produced in the 1960's.

Since 1969 the Beswick factory has been a part of Royal Doulton.

IDENTIFYING AND COLLECTING

The Equestrian figures have a shape number, name or breed either backstamped on the base or a plaque attached to the plinth.

Virtually all horses were produced in several colour variations, except the Connoisseur series. A decoration number identifies these colour variations; for instance 8760 was a brown gloss. In 1972 these numbers were changed to letters, but it is difficult to get an overall picture as there are many gaps in the price lists and catalogues still available.

Brown is the most common colour produced for well over 50 years. Also until 1984 all horse decorations varied in price with brown being the cheapest and grey being the most expensive. However, although you may see a lot of brown gloss Beswick horses on the market, it is worth checking if they are one of the shapes that were not issued in brown gloss for very long. Older examples have sharper mould details, nicely detailed eyes and pinkish tinges to the muzzled area.

To identify the horses you need knowledge of colour and finish variations. These can be the shape, colour and finish. For example it may be a current shape (they are still in production) but the colour and finish are both discontinued, making it a rarer piece, but not as rare as one completely discontinued.

The last Beswick catalogue was printed in 1988, and all figures produced after 1989 have the Royal Doulton backstamp.

The equestrian series are very sought after, for instance 'The Clowns on Horseback' (1950's) and the 'Thelwell' series (1980's).

Cheaper than Chips

B1. Mr Pricklepin
£110 €154

B2. Hunca Munca
(gold backstamp)
£125 €175

B3. Mrs Tittlemouse
£125 €175

B4. Cecily Parsley
£85 €119

B5. Samuel Whiskers
£90 €126

B6. Mrs Tiggywinkle
£65 €91

B7. Thomasina Ticklemouse
£100 €140

B8. The Head Gardener
(very rare)
£150 €210

B9. Squirrel Nutkin
£125 €175

B10. Mr. Benjamin
£60 €84

B11. Siamese kittens
£30 €42

B12. Charolais Calf
£90 €126

B13. Mr. Benjamin Bunny
'Peter Rabbit'
£90 €126

B14. Peter Rabbit
£125 €175

B15. Timmy Tiptoes
£125 €175

B16. Little Black Rabbit
£50 €70

B17. Squirrel flask
£20 €28

B18. Koala Bear
£40 €56

B19. Huntsman Fox
£34 €47

B20. Fisherman Otter
£34 €47

B21. Peter Rabbit
£50 €70

Cheaper than Chips

B22. Pigling Bland
£250 €350

B23. Mrs. Rabbit & Peter
(special edition)
£80 €112

B24. Fierce Bad Rabbit
£70 €98

B25. Peter Rabbit
gardening
£80 €112

B26. Seated cat
£24 €34

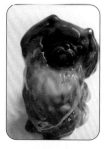

B27. Pekinese cat
£55 €77

B29. Scamp
£80 €112

B28. Tamworth Pig
£30 €42

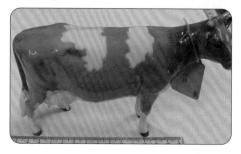

B30. Guernsey Cow
£145 €203

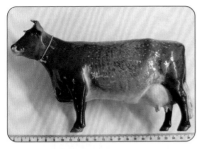

B31. Restored short horn cow
(perfect condition £1000)
£145 €**203**

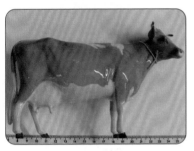

B32. Guernsey cow
1st version original
£400 €**560**

B33. Collie dog
£40 €**56**

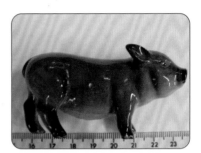

B34. Vietnamese
pot bellied pig
£20 €**28**

B35. Shirehorse foal
£34 €**47**

B36. Cat Musicians minatures set
(very collectable) **£190** €**252**

B37. Story time
Bunnykins
£33 €**46**

B38. Wall plate
£75 €**105**

B39. Ginger & Pickles
£150 €**210**

B40. Turtle Doves
£300 €**420**

Cheaper than Chips

B41. Barnacle Goose **£700** €980

B42. American Robin **£165** €231

B43. The Thrush **£80** €112

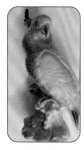

B44. Cockatoo (quite rare) **£150** €210

B45. Chaffinch **£20** €28

B46. Bullfinch **£20** €56

B47. Goldcrest **£20** €28

B48. Tourist Bunnykin (collectors club) **£65** €91

B49. Christmas plate **£30** €42

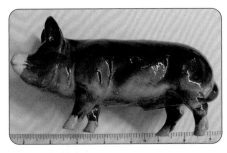

B50. Berkshire Boar (Rare breeds series) **£45** €**63**

B51. Middlewhite (Rare breeds series) **£45** €**63**

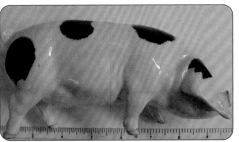

B52. Old Spot (Rare breeds series) **£45** €**63**

B56. Benjamin Bunny sat on a bank **£50** €**70**

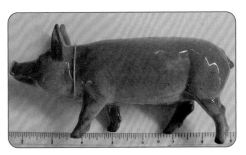

B53. Tamworth Sow rare breeds series **£45** €**63**

B54. Persian cat **£60** €**84**

B57. Mrs Tiggywinkle washing. (Ltd. Edition) **£80** €**112**

B55. Siamese cat **£65** €**91**

B58. Set of three comical Ducks **£80** €**112**

B59. Jemima Puddleduck **£50** e**70**

Cheaper than Chips

B60. Royal Doulton
Bunnykins bowl
£24 €**34**

B61. Appley Dapply
(very rare 1971 only)
£150 €**210**

B62. Timmy Willie
fetching milk
£25 €**35**

B63. Tom Kitten i
n the rockery
£50 €**70**

B64. Diggory Diggory
Velvet **£50** €**70**

B65. Peter in the
watering
can **£30** €**42**

B66. Mrs.
Tiggywinkle
£40 €**56**

B67. Mrs Rabbit
and Bunnies
£40 €**56**

B68. Appley Dapply
£150 €**210**

B69. Beswick cats
£35 €**49**

B70. Beswick white
cat **£35** €**49**

RA1. Mr. Jackson Royal Albert figure **£35** €**49**

RA2. Mother Ladybird circa 1989 **£40** €**56**

RA3. Royal Doulton Boy skater **£15** €**21** & Groom Bunnykins **£25** €**35**

RA4. R/A Jemima & Foxy **£50** €**70**

RA5. R/A Fox reading country news **£35** €**49**

RA6. Royal Doulton Mystic Bunnkins **£35** €**49**

RA7. R/A Peter with daffodils **£20** €**28**

RA8. R/A Badger **£55** €**77**

RA9. R/A Mrs Rabbit **£25** €**35**

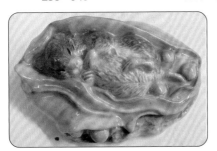

RA10. R/A Timmy Willie sleeping **£30** €**42**

RA11. R/A Goody Tiptoes **£45** €**63**

RA12. R/A Old woman knitting & Mrs Tittlemouse **£28** €**39**

Cheaper than Chips

RA13. R/A Gentleman mouse & Mrs Rabbit **£26** €**36**

RA14. R/A Sqirrel Nutkin **£25** €**35**

RA15. R/A Foxy whiskered gentleman **£25** €**35**

RA16. R/A Benjamin **£30** €**42**

RA17. R/A Pigling Bland **£22** €**31**

RA18. R/A Benjamin wakes up **£35** €**49**

RA19. R/A Ratty **£55** €**77**

RA20. R/A Peter and the red hankie **£28** €**39**

RA21. R/A Timmy Tiptoes **£45** €**63**

RA22. R/A Poorly Peter Rabbit **£25** €**35**

The Poole Potteries

In 1854 Thomas Ball and John Ridgeway along with Thomas and Frederick Saunders established the 'Patent Architectural Pottery' in Hamworthy (NR Poole). The company manufactured coloured and glazed bricks along with paving and wall tiles.

In 1861, the company's Forman; TW Walker left to set up his own pottery, but after a few years ran into financial difficulties and sold out to Jesse Carter (an iron monger) in 1873.

The company became known as Carter and Co. and continued with the production of mosaic work and tessellated tile pavements. These tiles were used in many commercial situations, for example pubs, diaries and baths. The tiles would often depict scenes of the Dorset countryside and subjects known as 'Old Bartholomew' and 'Fair/Little Dorrit'. Tiles would vary from 6" square to 1 1/6" square. The shapes would be square, diagonal and 1/2's of all shapes, along with strip boards and octagons.

The designs were bought in or by their own artists, one of the first being Edwin Page Turner whose half brother was James Radley Young, who was to figure largely in the development of the pottery.

By the 1880's the company began to be known locally as the Poole Potteries and was beginning to compete with companies such as Wedgwood.

William De Morgan bought many tile blanks in the late 1800's to experiment with glazes. He went on to design one of the first pieces recorded, it is marked Carter/Poole 2/1904 and is presently in the Victoria and Albert museum.

Owen Carter and Alfred Eason, who had previously worked at Spode and Minton, further developed glazing and finishing techniques.

At the turn of the century the company started to turn out more decorative pieces, such as vases, candlesticks, dishes, jardinieres and garden wares. They were contracted by Liberty & Co of London for balustrading, fountains, pergolas and large pots. Surviving identifiable pieces are in traditional Celtish style decorated with interlaced knots. On the commercial side the company continued to do work for pubs, expanding to sculptures; White Harts, Black Dogs etc.

Leading up to WW1 James Radley Young was head of the design department, and developed his passion for handmade decorative wares of Spanish and Portuguese design. He also developed modelling of figures, insects and reptiles and applied them to vases. During the war many restrictions were in place regarding the production of anything other than essential building materials. The company did however produce a range of commemorative wares featuring several wartime leaders on 8 1/4" plaques. Examples would be Gladstone, Kitchener and Lord Jellicoe.

By the 1920's the company had expanded under the name Carter, Stabler and Adams. The notable designers were Truda Carter, John Adams and both Harold and Phoebe Stabler. Truda Carter was the resident designer. Harold was a designer of gold and silver and Phoebe a pottery designer had in the past sold the design of 'The Picardy Peasant' (and others!) to both Poole and Doulton.

Lily Gilham (followed by her daughter Gertie who became chief thrower) was also an important name, as both a talented modeller and thrower, she was proficient in thin, fine wares, which all came out a little different.

She produced 3 main lines, 2 glazed and 1 unglazed. The earliest surviving pieces of the unglazed range are in coarse white clay (as used in tile production), with patterns inexpertly painted. There are examples of these in the Victoria and Albert Museum and the Poole Pottery LTD Collections. They are impressed with the Carter and Co. signature, indicating that the pottery was selling them very early on.

Out of the 2 glazed ranges, one heralded the later production of floral decorated pottery, which became Pooles most distinctive ware. This range was of flower sprigs with 2 or 3 colour motif petals, a stalk and a few leaves. Red or salmon coloured clay was used from the tile works, and then a number of glazes would be applied to the surface. Soluble colours were used in the painting, giving a soft, slightly fuzzy appearance.

'Blue stripe' was the other glazed range. Decoration ranged from plain stripes on the piece from top to bottom and sometimes a plain stripe around the rim, to elaborate diamonds and lozenges.

By the late 1920's the shape range had increased to include mugs, covered bowls and jars all with an increased finesse of production.

In the 1930's 'Plane ware' was developed which was mainly, if not all, vases which were plainly glazed and had flange type wings or handles. During this period the clay type also changed from the red clay (as the pits had run out) to a more white clay. This however is not an accurate guide to dating because of the density and variable colour of the white slip.

In 1931 a range of plates depicting boats of historical

interest was put in production. These were finely detailed pieces of vessels either built in Poole or used the harbour regularly.

Also around this time (1932) the number of glazes were increased to include the Picotee range with sprayed colours applied in rings around the body of the ware. These method of spraying was also used on the Everest ware, (which was both table and decorative), various coffee and tea sets designed by Harold Stabler including the 'Studland' range along with ornaments and figures.

In 1935 the 'Sylvian Glaze' range was used to describe a group of mottled colours with the codes M7, M22, M24, M36, M38, M70, M72. The colours ranged from black and orange, orange and yellow, yellow and green and yellow and blue. These colours were applied to existing shapes, vases, candle rings, ashtrays and inkstands.

The commercial tileworks continued throughout this period, influenced by the Stablers. They produced the War Memorial for Durban, South Africa and scenic mosaic commissions for food halls, The Hoover factory and London Underground. Other big commercial contracts carried out were The Queen Mary in 1932 and the Festival of Britain in 1951.

In the 1940's the plain cream / white ware became very popular, also the 'Twin tone' range, which was a 2 colour slip on all the pieces. There were 4 in all; sepia and mushroom, seagull and ice green, blue and magenta and peach bloom with seagull. Another notable range was the 'Sherbourne' a dinner and tea ware set, which was for export only up to 1950.

Truda Carter's wares continued under the new name of Traditional Poole, which were basically new designs or revamps of old.

In 1962 the company changed its name officially to Poole Pottery, and continued to produce new table ware designs, such as 'The Herb garden' (featuring Herbs) and 'Lucullus' featuring blackberry and apple, sweetcorn and other fruit and vegetables on different pieces of the range.

In 1964 Pilkington tiles bought out the tile works and eventually the Thomas Tilling Group absorbed the pottery works in 1971.

MARKS

The paintresses of 1922-1975 would have a 'mark' each of either their initials or a simple shape.

From 1900 - 1920 'Carters Poole' was signed on the base, rarely during this time do you see the circle with the dolphin in the center. In 1921 you rarely see an anchor being used. From 1925 - 1952 'Carter Stabler Adams Poole LTD' with or without a border, and from 1925-78 you see 'Poole England', again with or without boarders.

In the 1930's, wares that were part of a named range were generally printed with that name, in addition to the printed pattern or glaze code, impressed pottery back stamp, incised shape number and where applicable the paintresses insignia.

In 1952 a new stamp was introduced featuring the Dolphin insignia, along with 'Poole England'. Special wares also had 'Handmade, Hand decorated'.

In 1959 'Poole England' had a boarder, and in 1969 the addition of ovenproof, dishwasher safe etc was added. There are various themes of 'Poole England' featuring the dolphin used on traditional ware, craftware tableware and flatware.

10P. Table sweet dish 8 ins long
(200mm) **£35** €49

13P Vase 12" high **£50** €70

2P. Poole Vase 5ins (125mm) **£50** €70

1P. Bottom of picture 2P.

3P. Vase **£50** €70

4P. Two cups & saucers **£15** €21

5P. Two cups & saucers **£15** €21

6P. Vase 11ins high (250mm) **£45** €56

7P. Vase 6 ins high (150mm) **£38** €53

8P Vase 6 ins high (150mm) **£45** €63

9P. Vase 12 ins high (300mm) **£80** €112

Cheaper than Chips

11P. Vase 12 ins high
(300mm) **£44 €62**

12P. Bottom of 11P.

14P. Presentation plate
£60 €84

15P. Two Vases
£32 & £45 €45 & €63

16P. Small Vase
£40 €56

18P. Vase base
£30 €42

17P Vase 15 inches high
(375mm) **£40 €56**

19P. Vase
£45 €63

20P. Plate 7 inches
(175mm) **£10 €14**

25P. Flying machine series **£12** €**17**

21P. Scene of Dedham Mill by J.Constable & Plate each **£25** €**35**

22P. Reverse of Dedham Mill plate.

23P. D.Wallace designed plate **£10** €**14**

24P. Plates **£10** €**14 each**

26P. Flying machine series **£12** €**17**

27P. D.Wallace scene **£10** €**14**

28P. D.Wallace scene **£10** €**14**

Cheaper than Chips

29P. Hand painted plate **£35 €49**

30P. Seal scene **£15 €21**

31P. Poole Heritage year 1975 **£25 €35**

32P. Centre display **£13 €18**

33P. Vase 155mm high **£80 €112**

34P. Plate **£45 €63**

35P. Coffee Tea service individually priced **£5-£10 €7-€14**

37P. Table display **£30 €42**

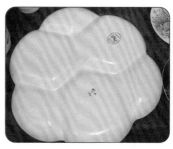

38P. Signed base of picture 37p.

Cheaper than Chips

36P. Modern dinner
service **£5 €7 each**

39P. Sauce boat **£8 €11**

40P Clarice Heath Vase
c.1937 **£110 €154**

41P. Winifred Collett Vase
£380 €532

42P. Miriam Heath Vase
£220 €308

43P. Nellie Bishton Vase
£375 €525

44P. Milk / Cream jug 6ins high
(150mm) **£145 €203**

45P. Jean Cockram Vase
£375 €525

46P. Miriam Heath Vase
£175 €245

Cheaper than Chips

48P. Jean Cockram Vase
£160 €224

49P. Betty Gooby Vase
£175 €245

50P. Miriam Heath Vase
£220 €308

51P. Miriam Heath Vase
£150 €210

52P. Jean Cockram Vase
£375 €525

53P. Poole wildlife collection prices
from **£40-£200 €56-€280**

54P. Poole wildlife collection
'Fox' **£175 €245**

55P Otter
£350 €490

56P. Small wildlife figures
£30-£70 €42-€98

57P. Fawn & Hedgehog
£70 €98

58P. White glazed Fish
£50-£150 €70-€210

59P. African savannah scene
Giraffe **£15 €21**

60P. Leopard
£15 €21

61P. Bison
£15 €21

62P. Gazelles
£15 €21

63P. Josephine Sydenham
Pot / vase
£65 €90

64P. Milk jug **£30 €42** & Josephine
Sydenham Vase **£25 €35**

65P. Josephine Sydenham
Vase **£80 e112**

66P. Hilda Hampton
Vase **£200 €280**

Cheaper than Chips

67P. Small Myrtle Bond dish **£40** €**56**

68P. Sugar bowl & cover **£15** €**21**

69P. Miriam Heath Vase **£220** €**308**

70P. Miriam Heath Vase **£150** €**210**

71P. Jean Cockram Vase **£375** €**525**

72P. Josephine Sydenham Vase **£95** €**133**

73P. Doris Marshall Vase **£375** €**525**

74P. Iris Downton Vase **£150** €**210**

75P. Vase **£225** €**315**

76P. Small jug by Irene Hayes **£70** €**98**

Cheaper than Chips

86P. Pair eggcups **£55 €77**

Thimbles and treasures of the Needlework Box can easily be found at any car-boot sale or antique fair. For some strange reason when you think how widely these items were used just 50 years ago. They are not highly valued by many. I don't know why this is as there were many fine examples produced from scissors, cotton reels, bobbins, tape measures and needle holders.

(Continued on Page 260)

77P. Nellie Bishton Vase **£375 €525**

78P Cream / Milk / Water jugs **£35 £250 £55 €49 €350 €77**

79P. Collection of Thimbles **£5 €7 each**

80P. Vase **£375 €525**

81P. Miriam Heath Vase **£175 €245**

82P. Experimental trial lustre **£60 €84**

83P. Set Table ware **£75 €105**

84P Set Table ware **£65 €91**

85P Egg cup **£45 €63**

Cheaper than Chips

87P. Gwen Haskins Pot
£80 €**112**

88P. Tony Morris plate
£340 €**476**

89P. 1930's Milk jug **£180** €**252** &
Anne Hatchard jug **£350** €**490**

90P Cosmic pattern living glaze
£45-£70 €**63-**€**98**

91P Deborah Farrance
pot **£85** €**119**

92P. Gladys Hallett Urn
£375 €**525**

93P. Jaqueline Way
Egg cup **£50** €**77**

94P. Vase **£**
230 €**322**

95P. Hand painted plate
8 inch (200mm) **£65** €**90**

(Continued from Page 259)

Very exquisitely decorated with gold, silver, ebony, ivory or mother of pearl, any Victorian lady would have a large collection and they would have more often than not be handed down through generation after generation. Start collecting!

96P. Hand painted plate
5 inch (125mm) **£45** €**63**

97P. Hand painted plate
4 inch (100mm) **£30** €**42**

98P. Hand painted plate
4 inch (100mm) **£30** €**42**

99P. Hand painted plate
8 inch (200mm) **£65** €**90**

100P. Hand painted plate
8 inch (200mm) **£65** €**90**

101P. Stoneware by
Barbara Lindley Adams
'Otter' **£340** €**476**

102P. Stoneware Falcon
£300 €**420**

103P. Stoneware Dog
£280 €**392**

104P. Stoneware Grouse
£280 €**392**

105P. Tony Harris Dragon Fly
design **£325** €**455**

Cheaper than Chips

106P Season Plaques left Summer, right Autumn **£60** €**84**

107P. Back of Autumn plaque.

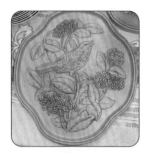

108P. Season plaque Summer **£60** €**84**

109P. Season plaque Spring **£60** €**84**

110P. Season plaque Winter **£60** €**84**

111P. Back of Winter plaque.

112P. Two small serving dishes **£9** €**13**

113P Poole craft Dolphin **£16** €**22**

114P. White glazed Fish **£50-£150** €**70-€210**

115P. Siamese Cats
£70 €**90**

116P Brooch 10/500
Ltd Edition **£65** €**91**

117P. Back of picture 116P.

118P. Johanna Rolf plate
£55 €**77**

119P. Sleeping puppies
£60 €**84 each**

120P. Badger
£70 €**90**

121P. Puppy
£60 €**84**

122P. Field Mouse with
strawberry **£60** €**84**

123P. Melbury pattern Coffee / Tea set
£40-£60 €**56-€84**

124P. Stoneware sculptures
£100-£300 €**140-€420**

Cheaper than Chips

125P. Fawn
£80 €112

126P. Duck
£100 €140

128P. Mice / Squirrel
£45-£60 €63-€84

127P. Owl
£350 €490

129P. Hamster & Tortoise
£80 €112

130P. Fawn
£45 €63

131P. Glazed Bowls
£8 €11

132P. Lamb
£30 €42

133P. Pair Dolphins
£40 €56

134P. Devon County plate **£40** €**56**

135P. Plate
£18 €**25**

136P. Kittens
£18 €**25**

137P. Kitten & puppy
£18 €**25**

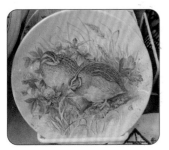

138P. Grouse
£18 €**25**

139P. Winter scene
£18 €**25**

140P. Princess & Frog
£18 €**25**

141P. Flowers
£18 €**25**

142P. Lady & Car
£20 €**28**

143P. County plate Wiltshire & Berkshire **£40** €**56**

Cheaper than Chips

144P. Womens Institute 1918-1968 Golden Jubilee **£40 €56**

145P. Poole Harbour / Brownsea Island **£40 €56**

146P. Rare Red body impressed C.S.A. by Anne Hatchard **£900 €1260**

147P. Rare small figure 'Flower seller' circa. 1928 **£380 €532**

148P. Picture of base of 'Flower seller'.

149P. Water jug **£40 €56**

150P. Anita Harris trial plate star sign 'Gemini' **£75 €105**

151P. Anita Harris trial plate star sign 'Leo' **£75 €105**

Ask

If there are things you are not sure of the golden rule is to ask - the majority of people at auctions and carboot sales are there because they are enthusiasts too; share your own knowledge and learn from others. You will probably find the experts on hand will love to talk about their passion for antiques.

Being educated by those on the 'shop floor' is invaluable and cannot be replicated by any book - everyone has a story to tell about their journey through a world of antiques.

462. Pair of binoculars in leather case **£30** €**42**

463. Carved oak wall barometer damaged **£50** €**70**

464. Pair cast iron flower troughs **£100** €**140**

465. Walnut coal Purdonium **£40** €**56**

466. Flute in case **£50** €**70**

470. Two pewter tankards and one pot **£30** €**42**

467. Inside flute case picture 466.

469. Two carved oak wall barometers **£50 each** €**70 each**

468. Cast brass two bottle ink stand **£40** €**56**

Cheaper than Chips

D1. 4 alloy wheels (Vauxhall)
£30 €42

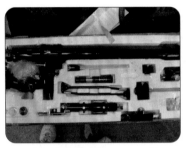

D2. Boxed telescope and attachments A/F
£20 €28

D3. Brass ships oil lamp
£30 €42

D4. 3 plumbers blow torches
£15 €21

D5. Original brass stick telephone
£45 €63

D6. 2 Lorna Bailey china cats
£60 €84

D7. Three spirit bottles
£20v28

D8. Early wind-up gramophone A/F
£50 €70

D9. Masons part tea service
£50 €70

D10. Philips VHF/AM electric radio
£15 €21

D11. Oriental copper measuring jug
£20 €28

D12. 2 copper measuring jugs
£30 €42

Royal Worcester (Figurines) HISTORY

Dr John Wall started the Worcester Tonquin Manufacture in 1751, the beginning of the oldest continually existing porcelain manufacturer in Britain.

With William Davis, Wall developed a soft paste method of making porcelain, which would not crack when brought into contact with boiling water. This recipe has remained largely unchanged over the last 250 years. The first designs were teapots and tableware, which quickly surpassed other manufacturer sales.

Figurines did not come into production at Worcester until the 1760's, later that other porcelain factories in Bow, Chelsea and Derby. These factories had started to produce a number of figurines based on the continental models, whilst Worcester concentrated on quality tableware.

When the Bristol plant merged with Worcester (1752) they made a few basic figurines such as white glazed Chinese man, and a figure 'Cupid at Vulcan's Forge' (1760's), which was thought to be modelled by John Toulouse, who also made other figurines.

William Davis took over the management of the factory in 1776 until his death in 1783, then the company's London agent Thomas Flight, purchased the company.

The company was awarded the Royal Warrant in 1789. This followed a visit to the factory by King George III and Queen Charlotte. This is where the term Royal Worcester first came into use, and Royal Warrants have been enjoyed by the factories ever since.

Flight, along with his sons John and Joseph, and various family members ran the company factory at Worcester until the 1840's, selling mostly tableware. Around this time Royal Worcester took over the Chamberlains factory at Diglis, where the present day factory stands.

In 1852 the company changed hands again, bought by WH Kerr and RW Binns (the Kerr and Binns period) The new owners introduced Parian, a new material first used in the 1840's, to the Worcester factory. The result was a more lasting and easily coloured and guilded product, making it suitable for the more detailed modelling that made Royal Worcester's name.

This lead to a greater demand and expansion in production of figurines, especially when the company issued stock and started trading as the Royal Worcester LTD. in 1862.

At this time the company started to hire trained sculptors, the most important names in this period were W. Boyton, E.J. Jons and C. Toft. W.B. Kirk was responsible for modelling many class 1 busts and class 2 figurines, and some carry his name moulded on the body.

Important painters at the time were David Bates who specialized in flowers and Birkett Foster - subjects, Steven Lawton who did enamel decorations, Robert Perling who worked on Landseer subjects, Josiah Rushton on human figures and Luke Wells on animals.

The 1870s saw James Hadley producing the greatest number and variety of styles of Worcester models. He developed the Japanesque style (copies of the Japanese work at the time) which was often so good it was copied by the Japanese themselves. He also worked on, most notably, the Middle Eastern figures and Countries of the world series; also Persian, Indian and Italian 'renaissance' styles.

Hadley left Royal Worcester in 1876 to start his own company in 1896. After his death Hadleys' Company was amalgamated with the Royal Worcester Company.

Around 1860-1870 Royal Worcester produced a lot of 'gimmicky' castings. Such as a model of a dog whose head would lift off to become a matchbox, menu holders in the style of popular (and un-popular) politicians of the day. Also produced were some quite humorous pieces of the Victorian period.

Due to the increasing popularity of the Royal Worcester name they experienced some 'copy cat' factories in the area. After a court battle, a judge ruled that only Royal Worcester could carry the name Worcester on their pieces. The two other factories were Locke and Co. and James Hadley and Sons.

In the early 1900s a few animal figures were produced, often modelled by the Evans family. During the war Royal Worcester produced some delicate porcelain figures, imitating those produced in Germany in an attempt to replace German goods for British ones.

Frederick M Gertner produced the highly accurate 'Historical' and 'Regimental' series.

Around this time a number of small, nude models of boys and girls also appeared. These were fashioned in Crown Ware, a much cheaper product than Parian to produce. This attempt to increase sales did nothing for the factory and it went into receivership in 1930. Two weeks later it reopened under the direction of Joseph Grimson, who pushed the factory back into the high quality figures, and over the next few years produced over ninety new figurines.

Only during the Second World War and the blitz have they come close to halting production since.

In 1941 Eileen Soper modelled the 'Wartime' series; it

was not popular and these pieces are hard to find in today's market.

Over the following years successful modellers have included Stella Crofts, Doris Linder ('Equestrian'series) andGwendolen Parnell ('Cries of London' series) to name a few.

Dorothy Doughty modelled the popular 'Birds' series, Freda Doughty modelled the childrens series, such as 'Nursery Rhyme', 'Months of the year', 'Children of the Nations' and 'Days of the Week' which, lauched in the 1930's, is still in production today.

COLLECTING ROYAL WORCESTER

Many pieces are part of a series or a pair, which work well together. Other people collect by painter, modeller, or period, the choice of pieces has grown very large over the years.

REGISTRATIONS,BACKSTAMPS & DATING

THE basic marking system of four linked W's on a Crown originated in 1862, with the Royal Worcester England appearing around the crest from 1891.

Many early Royal Worcester shape numbers are incised on the base of the subject. Some of the early trade marks and diamond shape registration marks are moulded (produced on a pad raised above the surface of the base).

Other factories imitating the style used similar marks. Most of the printed marks since 1862 have an elaborate system of year mark codes, and a greater understanding of these will help your knowledge of the wares. The coding can be very complicated with dates, letters in upper and lower case and the addition or deletion of the word England. From 1892-1915 a series of dots on either side of the crown would represent the year, after 1916 a system using an * with dots on either side came into use.

After 1927 three interlaced circles with increasing dots were used, in the 1940's letters started being used and in 1963 a shape or pattern was introduced instead of the codes.

There is a Royal Worcester collectors' society, based out of Worcester.

481. Lladro figure of girl and dog **£30 €42**

D13. Box of armorial ware
£30 €42

D14. Sylvac planter and jugs
£15 €21

D15. Pair Lorna Bailey Lava pattern condiments & Moorland vase
£40 €56

D16. 3 items of cream ware
£15 €21

D17. 4 Majolica plates and comports
£30 €42

D20. Victorian pattern dinner service
£45 €63

D18. 3 Royal Worcester serving dishes
£35 €49

D19. 3 Carlton ware leaf dishes & jug
£30 €42

D21. Collection of limited edition 'Fairy' scene plates
£40 €56

Cheaper than Chips

471. Knife cleaner
£40 €56

472. Victorian ebonised pearlshell
inkstand **£30 €42**

474. Perpetual Calendar /
date display **£50 €70**

473. Pair soap stone carved
monkeys **£40 €56**

476. Company stamp
£30 €42

477. Brass pan/ log bin
£30 €42

478. Violin in case
£50 €70

475. Copper Tea kettle on stand
with burner **£50 €70**

479. Base of picture 480
Moorland jug.

480. Moorland jug
£40 €56

Papier Mâché

If you can tear yourself away from the vision of an infant plastered in glue and paper destroying your best table, it has actually been around since Henry Clay, a Birmingham Japanner who patented it in 1772 as 'Clay Ware'. It was either pulped and poured into moulds or sheets or glued paper pressed together. Light, versatile and strong it was very popular with the Victorians after it was lavishly shown in many forms from snuffboxes to tables, chairs, wardrobes and even beds. Easily

(Continued on Page 273.)

Cheaper than Chips

decorated with paint, gilt or inlay, for around 50 years since the great exhibition of 1851 it was virtually the plastic of the Victorians.

D24. Oriental Kukri knife
£25 €35

D22. Metal Knight in armour table lighter
£20 €28

D23. Oriental carved resin figure 'Bird'
£30 €42

D25. Ornate 3 bottle ink stand
£20 €28

D27. 8 day Swiss travelling clock
£30 €42

D26. Early 20c Mahogany fishing reel
£40 €56

D28. Cast brass silver on gilt bottle ink stand
£30 €42

D29. Early 20c school hand bell
£30 €42

D30. Brass microscope, good quality
£60 €84

D31. London-Midland railway engine light £70 €98

D32. Railway carriage rear light
£35 €49

D33. Copper railway carriage lamp
£50 €70

D34. Composite Negro dolly
£40 €56

Cheaper than Chips

482. Poole pottery vase
£50 €70

483. Moorland jug
£30 €42

LM07. Wade teapot English life
'The Antique shop'
£15 €21

485. Moorland sugar sifter
£35 €49

486. Hand painted pottery
picture of 487.

487. Two Poole Pottery cups
and saucers **£15 €21**

488. Etched decanter and
stopper **£15 €21**

489. Moorland vase
£35 €49

490. Pair of Japanese style
vases **£15 €21**

491. Poole Pottery vase
£45 €56

Making Assumptions

If you are making a decision to purchase an expensive item, get your facts right. Never make assumptions as to the authenticity, condition or quality of antiques. If in doubt ask, inspect and don't agree to purchase until you are sure. In the case of less expensive items where you are not sure of these issues, it may be worth a gamble but only if you are prepared to win some and lose some.

D35. Composite bodied doll
£40 €56

D36. Composite bodied doll
£40 €56

D37. Composite doll with jointed arms/legs
£45 €63

D38. Well loved 1940's teddy
£50 €70

D39. Straw filled soft toy duck
£50 €70

D40. Carlton ware preserves pot & lid
£25 €35

D41. Royal Doulton figure 'The news vendor'
£140 €196

D42. 300mm high Moorcroft vase
£160 €224

D43. Wedgewood figure
£30 €42

D44. 200mm Moorcroft jar & cover
£155 €217

D45. Macintyre jug 320mm high
£340 €476

D46. Moorcroft bowl 150mm wide
£120 €168

Cheaper than Chips

D47. Sylvac vase
£15 €21

D48. Pair of Royal
Doulton dogs
£30 €42

D49. Moorcroft pot
& cover
£140 €196

D50. Lladro figure girl
picking flowers
£45 €63

D51. Lladro figure
'Boy yawning
£35 €49

D53. Early Moorcroft
vase 250mm high
£350 €490

D54. 2 Wedgewood black
jasper ware trinket boxes
£20 €28

D52. Limoges hand
painted trinket box
£40 €56

D55. Copeland Spode
soap dish & cover
£25 €35

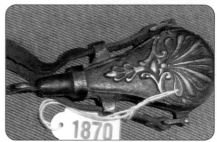

D56. Middle eastern lime
flask & screw stopper
£50 €70

Cheaper than Chips

Meccano

D58. Meccano E15R electric motor
£50 €70

Meccano was once the 'must have' toy of the 1930's right through to the 1970's. Some boxed sets can fetch hundreds of pounds. The complete sets of boxed Meccano are a nostalgic collector's dream and will also increase in value. You will always see the odd bit or box full of Meccano at an auction or car boot sale, so do yourself a favour and start picking up pieces cheaply!!

boxed with instructions
£200 €280

D59. Tower steam factory
£50 €70

D60. DC steam factory
£70 €98

D61. Scratch built steam factory
£70 €98

D62. Moorcroft vase 150mm
£140 €196

D63. Poole pottery vase
£40 €56

D64. Wedgewood green Majolica leaf plate
£35 €49

D65. Royal Doulton character jug 'Samuel Johnson'
£160 €224

D66. Poole pottery vase
£40 €56

D67. Pair Sarreguemines tureens & covers
£40 €56

Cheaper than Chips

D69. Royal Doulton salt-glazed stoneware jug
£38 €53

D70. Victorian blue & white vase
£32 €45

D71. Mason Ironstone blue & white jug
£100 €140

D72. Royal Doulton salt-glazed stoneware jug
£70 €98

D68. Staffordshire B/W motto cup & saucer
£35 €49

D73. Royal Doulton figure of 'The Winner' horse
£40 €56

D74. Continental figure of 2 lovers
£70 €98

D75. 2 Carlton ware dishes
£35 €49

D77. Boxed grey top hat & gloves
£40 €56

D78. Studio design jugs & mugs
£20 €28

D79. Staffordshire figure group
£40 €56

John Shelly

Production of Shelly pieces date back to the late 1940's and operated both in the Dorset and Devon area over the next 20 years, producing studio pottery. It is very collectable today, a good piece can cost hundreds of pounds so if you come across a mark J over an S on a piece of cream ware, which became popular tourist pieces in the 1950's and 1960's and exported all over the world, it could be your lucky day!

D76. 2 Carlton ware dishes
£35 €49

D80. Mamod working
steam model of DV1
£120 €168

D81. Shelly toilet
jug & bowl
£120 €168

D82. 2 coloured glass
bowls & covers
£80 €112

D83. Old Bank of England
£5 note
£25 €35

D84. Copper & leather
powder & shot flask
£50 €70

D85. Turned wood
& brass Flute
£100 €140

D86. Turned ivory
box & cover
£40 €56

D87. Pewter
Inkwell & pen stand
£30 €42

D88. Enamelled
fish pattern box
£30 €42

Cheaper than Chips

D89. 3 enamelled
miniature bowls
£20 €28

D90. Patinated & gilt
cast alloy figure
£40 €56

D91. Edwardian mahogany
mantel clock
£120 €168

D92. Early 20c
Mannequin
£80 €112

D93. Two glass
washing boards
£30 €42

D94. Bronze figure of Ballerina
emerging from a shell
£160 €22

D95. Bronze figure
'After Schiparus'
£160 €224

D96. Folded Peacock style
face fire-guard
£35 €49

D97. Box of miniature
Liqueur bottles
£20 €28

D98. Walt Disney
'Micky Mouse' tea pot
£80 €112

Investments

If you want to make an investment for the future do your homework. It is not worth collecting mass, produced memorabilia regardless of its popularity now. Buy what is rare, not popular.

493. Brass dinner gong
£15 €21

492. Ice cream maker
£20 €28

494. Two Hummel
figures **£20 €28**

495. Cast statue
figures
£20 €28

501. Three Bells whisky
bottles **£30 €42**

496. Six gnome figures
£10 €14

497. Signed base of Lorna Bailey
jug picture 498.

498. Lorna Bailey jug, 'House
and Path' **£40 €56**

499. Pottery jardiniere
£10 €14

502. Moorland 'Leopard'
tea pot **£40 €56**

504. Lorna Bailey bird
figure **£75 €104**

503. Base of picture
504 Lorna Bailey.

Cheaper than Chips

NC88. Sylvac planter
£14 €19

NC89. Old milk urn (hung on back of cart)
£58 €81

NC90. Keele street pottery
£10 €14 & £14 €19

NC91. Old gramophone
£40 €56

NC92. Victorian coal iron
£24 €33

NC93. Ovaltine jubilee mug
£8 €11

NC94. Black dolly
£20 €28

HY28. Early 20c metal & Bakelite cutlery
£20 €28

NC96. Wade treasure chest
£8 €11

Cheaper than Chips

Trust Your Instincts

If you are not sure of authenticity, condition or value, then trust your instincts. If you are in doubt, wait and see how the item goes; if there are a few bidders and the price keeps going up steadily, then there is a good chance it is what it appears to be.

505. Three Blue china cats **£20** €28

506. Novelty tea pot, 'Fishmongers' **£15** €21

507. Novelty tea pot **£15** €21

508. Wind-up gramophone **£85** €119

509. Brass tea kettle on stand **£45** €63

510. Three pieces coloured glass **£10** €14

511. Pair of oriental vases **£10** €14

LM04. Wade English life teapot 'China shop' **£10** €14

513. Lorna Bailey figure of a cat **£40** €56

Cheaper than Chips

NC01. Calyx ware
£5 €7

NC02. Royal Doulton
Posy
£13 €18

NC03. Crown Staffordshire
Tortoise
£5 €7

NC04. Heathercoat Hall
posy **£10 €14**

NC05. Travelling jewellery
box, leather
£12 €17

NC06. Wood ware lidded cup
£7 €10

NC07. Midwinter
special edition
£40 €56

NC08. Sylvac dish **£6**
€9

NC09. Bone china
miniature tea set
£20 €28

Wood - Arthur

Established in 1928 at the Bradwell works in Longport, Staffordshire, Arthur Wood produced a wide range of lightly decorated earthen ware, not terribly expensive in today's market. They produced some very nice pieces where single items look good in their own right and are easily identified by a globe with the name Arthur Wood across the middle.

NC10. Sadler celery vase **£10** €**14**

NC11. Alfred Meakin marigold 'Astoria' shape **£6** €**9**

NC12. Arthur Wood bowl **£12** €**17**

NC13. Staffordshire jug **£16** €**22**

NC14. Dinky toy 'Shadow 2' **£8** €**11**

NC15. Corgi car transporter **£8** €**11**

NC16. Wedgewood Peter Rabbit dish **£6** €**9**

NC17. Lustre glass pot **£7** €**10**

NC18. Peter Rabbit soap dish and soap **£5** €**7**

NC19. Denby jug **£10** €**14**

Cheaper than Chips

NC20. Mason 'Formosa' dish
£10 €14

NC21. Cornish kitchen ware T.G. Green
£25 €35

NC22. Leather holster and replica gun
£75 €105

NC23. 9ct Gold jewellery
£38 €53

NC24. Silver gilt and Garnet earrings
£22 €31

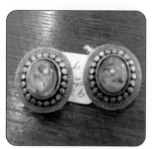

NC25. Silver and Amber earrings
£10 €14

NC26. Crystal earrings
£8 €11

NC27. Silver and Amethyst earrings
£12 €17

NC28. Silver and Onyx earrings
£8 €11

Jewellery

There is no doubt that through the Victorian era the jewellery market exploded, mainly because of the huge range of new materials that came onto the market from around the world. The industrial age brought enormous wealth to a much larger portion of the population and cameos, brooches, bracelets and earrings came onto a virtually barren market for the masses.

Precious stones, quartz, amber and jade were produced quite cheaply and often set in silver or gilt metal. Not only are some of these pieces quite acceptable in their own right

(Continued on Page 287)

Cheaper than Chips

as jewellery but many contain quite rare stones. Human hair was often introduced into pieces for memorial purposes and these would be highly decorated. So please take good advice before letting any pieces go. Valuations on pieces you are unsure about are cheap and a valuation service is offered by most jewellers for insurance purposes.

NC29. Chinese Quartz earrings **£8 €11**

NC30. Silver and Amber earrings **£12 €17**

NC31. 9ct Gold and Citrine earrings **£32 €45**

NC32. 9ct Gold and cameo earrings **£38 €53**

NC33. Ruby cross earrings **£6 €9**

NC34. 18ct Gold and Sapphire **£48 €67**

NC35. Silver pill box **£15 €21**

NC36. Silver pill box **£12 €17**

NC37. Pad of Early 20c. Art Nouveau brooches **£10 €14 to £40 €56**

NC38. Victorian Scottish silver **£28 €39**

Cheaper than Chips

NC39. Marcasite, Onyx
and Kingfisher
£9 €5 & £12 €7

NC40. Silver brooch
£10 €14

NC41. Silver and Marconite
£20 €28

NC42. Metal bracelet
£10 €14

NC43. Metal and glass
brooch
£9 €12

NC44. Victorian
cameo brooch
£45 €63

NC45. Early 20c glass bead
brooch
£8 €11

NC46. Metal and
transfer brooch
£8 €11

NC47. 9ct Gold cameo
brooch
£32 €45

Cameos

Cameos and painted brooches enjoy a healthy market. They were very popular right up to the late 1960's. The Victorian era brought about the production of the finest mass produced pieces, and although many were transfer printed, good quality items were also produced in vast numbers. These were made using ivory, wood and precious stones and some would have been hand painted, all of which are collectable and valuable.

Even if you do not have any of these be assured that most brooches and cameos attract attention at the car boot sale if they are good quality and of a certain age.

Cheaper than Chips

NC48. Sterling silver and enamel brooch
£16 €22

NC49. Two silver eggs cups
£25 €35 each

NC50. Rolled gold bracelet
£16 €22

NC51. Mosaic box
£8 €11

NC52. Silver powder compact **£28 €39**

NC53. Victorian locket **£28 €39**

NC54. 9ct White gold and diamond **£55 €77**

NC55. Cloisonné bangle
£10 €14

NC56. Chinese carved ivory stool, 125mm
£28 €39

NC57. Trinket box
£8 €11

Cheaper than Chips

NC58. Mosaic pill box
£10 €14

NC59. Crown Staffordshire posy
£8 €11

NC60. Clocking in machine
£65 €91

NC61. Pair Royal Doulton vases 125mm high
£30 €42

NC62. Clarice Cliff bowl
£70 €98

NC63. Base of Clarice Cliff bowl NC62.

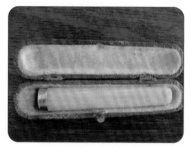

NC64. Amber & gold cigarette holder
£26 €36

NC65. Royal Winton dish 140mm
£10 €14

NC66. Royal Winton dish old cottage chintz
£10 €14

NC67. Embroidery handbag/purse
£12 €17

Cheaper than Chips

Buyer's Premium

Be aware that auction houses will charge a premium per lot to sell as well as a buyer's premium of 15-20%. This is the usual, but can vary.

514. Lorna Bailey
wall pocket
£45 €63

517. Base of picture 514
Lorna Bailey

516. Lorna Bailey salt and pepper
& Moorland tea pot **£45 each**
€63 each

LM06. Wade teapot
English life 'The Pub'
£10 €14

518. Poole pottery vase
£38 €53

519. Royal Doulton character jug
Scaramouche **£70 €98**

520. Three Wade Flying
Toucans **£50 €70**

521. Old brass & wood
telephone (feature)
£20 €28

522. Royal Doulton figure
Jennifer **£85 €119**

523. Royal Doulton figures
Adrienne and Hannah
£90 each €126 each

Cheaper than Chips

NC68. Porcelain shamrock
£14 €19

NC69. Pair modern
perfume bottles
£7 €10 each

NC70. Early 20c Toby jugs
£48 €67

NC71. Coppercraft
Staffordshire cow
£32 €45

NC72. Coppercraft
Staffordshire cow
£32 €45

NC73. Miniature Wade items
£2 €3

NC74. Miniature Wade items
£2 €3

NC75. Chinese hand
painted bottles
£20 €28 each

NC76. Aynsley knife
£10 €14

531. Lladro 'Three singing cherubs' **£80** €**112**

524. Royal Doulton figures
Elaine and Sharon
£90 each €126 **each**

LM09. The Leonardo collection
'Cottage' teapot
£15 €**21**

526. Royal Doulton
peregrine falcon
£100 €**140**

527. Royal Doulton
figure **£35** €**49**

528. Two cut glass inkwells & Vaseline
scent bottle **£30 £45** €**42** €**63**

LM10. Wade English life teapot
'Christmas tree'
£10 €**14**

530. 19c. Staffordshire match stand
& Royal Doulton jug 'Viking'
£30 £35 €**42** €**49**

532. Two Wedgewood boxes
and covers **£20** €**28**

Cheaper than Chips

Notes